The Body Ma

CW01590114

Contents

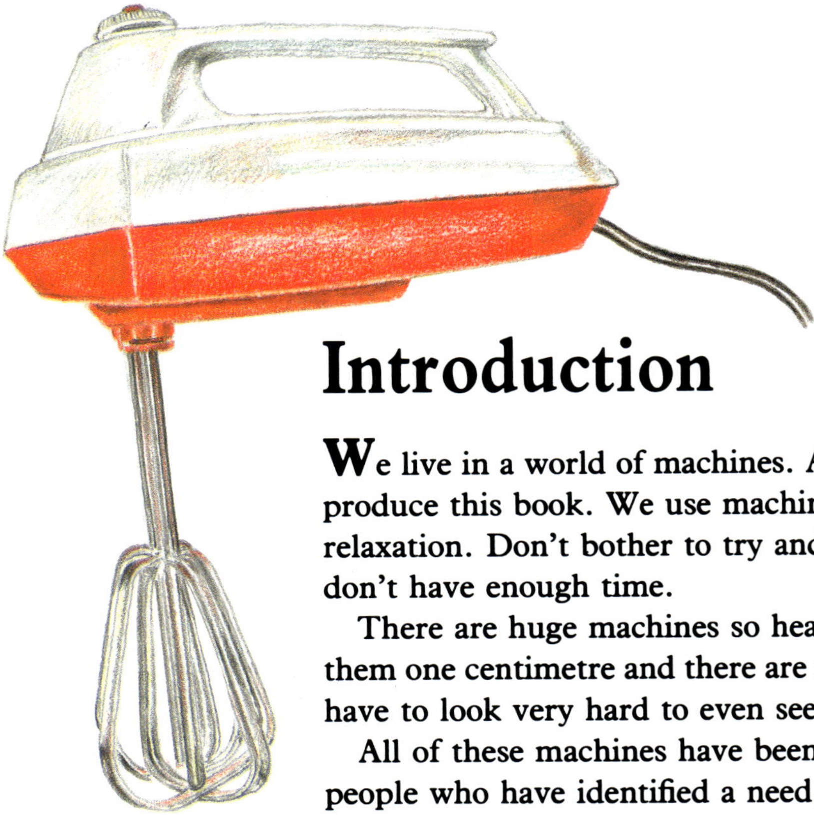

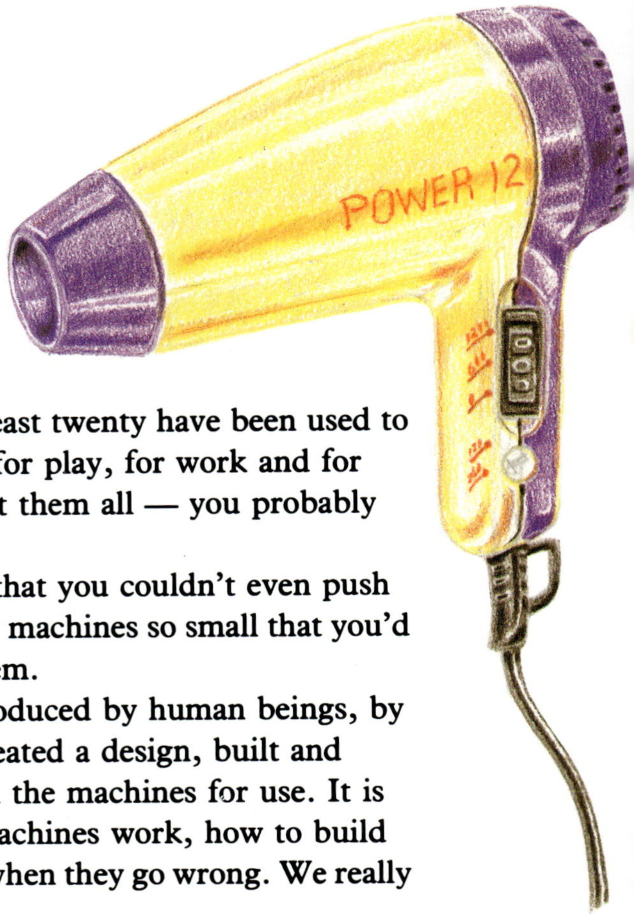

Introduction

We live in a world of machines. At least twenty have been used to produce this book. We use machines for play, for work and for relaxation. Don't bother to try and list them all — you probably don't have enough time.

There are huge machines so heavy that you couldn't even push them one centimetre and there are tiny machines so small that you'd have to look very hard to even see them.

All of these machines have been produced by human beings, by people who have identified a need, created a design, built and improved on the design and produced the machines for use. It is possible to know exactly how these machines work, how to build more of them and how to repair them when they go wrong. We really do live in a 'machine age'.

There is one machine, though, that is different from all the machines you might see around you. It's a machine so complicated, so exciting, so thought-provoking and so useful that you can't do without it.

It's your body.

Your body machine can work on its own without any conscious command. (How many times a day do you stop to tell your heart to carry on beating?) When your body machine breaks down it can often repair itself. (Just think what happens when you cut your knee.) Your body machine links hundreds of different parts and

enables them to work together. (Can it really be only your eyes which are working while you read this?) Your body machine can do hundreds and hundreds of different jobs, more than almost any other machine. (Just try listing everything your body machine does today.)

But of course, your body machine also grows old and tired, less able to do the range of things it has done in the past. That's why your grandpa or grandma might be a little slower than you, a little less able to run very fast through the park. In the end, you can't do much about this and your body machine will wear out like all machines. But by exercising, eating good food whenever you can and not doing anything which you know will harm the way your body machine works, you can help to keep it in good condition for a long, long time.

This book is all about your body machine. We hope some of the things in it will amaze you and we know you will learn lots about how your body works. Above all, though, we hope it will help you realize what a fantastic machine you are. Take care of yourself!

The human skeleton

Our bodies are made of flesh and blood built on a framework of bones. Without our bones, we could not stand up or move about. We would be as floppy as a suit of clothes without a hanger. But we do not stand stiffly like shop-window models or big solid statues. We can walk, jump, run and wiggle our toes because our bodies are made up of a great many separate bones all joined together by stretchy bands of muscle.

Some of the bones are actually joined together so that they cannot be moved individually. This gives them extra strength. Your skull, for example, is made up of 30 flattened bones which interlock like a jigsaw. Others meet at movable joints which are like hinges and make us flexible, supple and bendy. Each of us has about 206 bones of all shapes and sizes and over 600 muscles.

As well as allowing us to move, our bones and muscles protect the very important organs inside our bodies. A cage of ribs encloses the heart and lungs. A box-like skull protects the brain. A cord of nerves runs safely up through the centre of the spine bones. The hip bones and spine shield the liver, intestines and stomach.

Look at one of your hands. Can you see and feel the different bones in it?

- Place your hand on a plain piece of paper and draw around it.
- Try and draw in the different bones that you can feel.
- Model your finger bones and the way they move using pipe-cleaners and straws. Cut the straws to match the length of the individual finger bones.
- Thread the straw pieces on the pipe-cleaners and join them all together.

You can try feeling and modelling other bones in your body too.

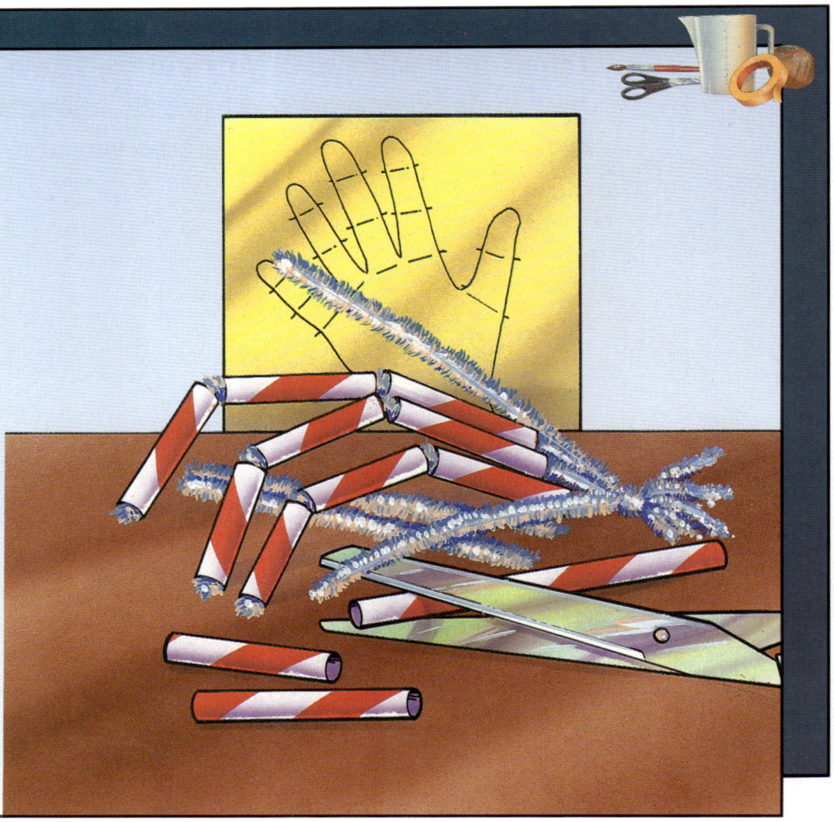

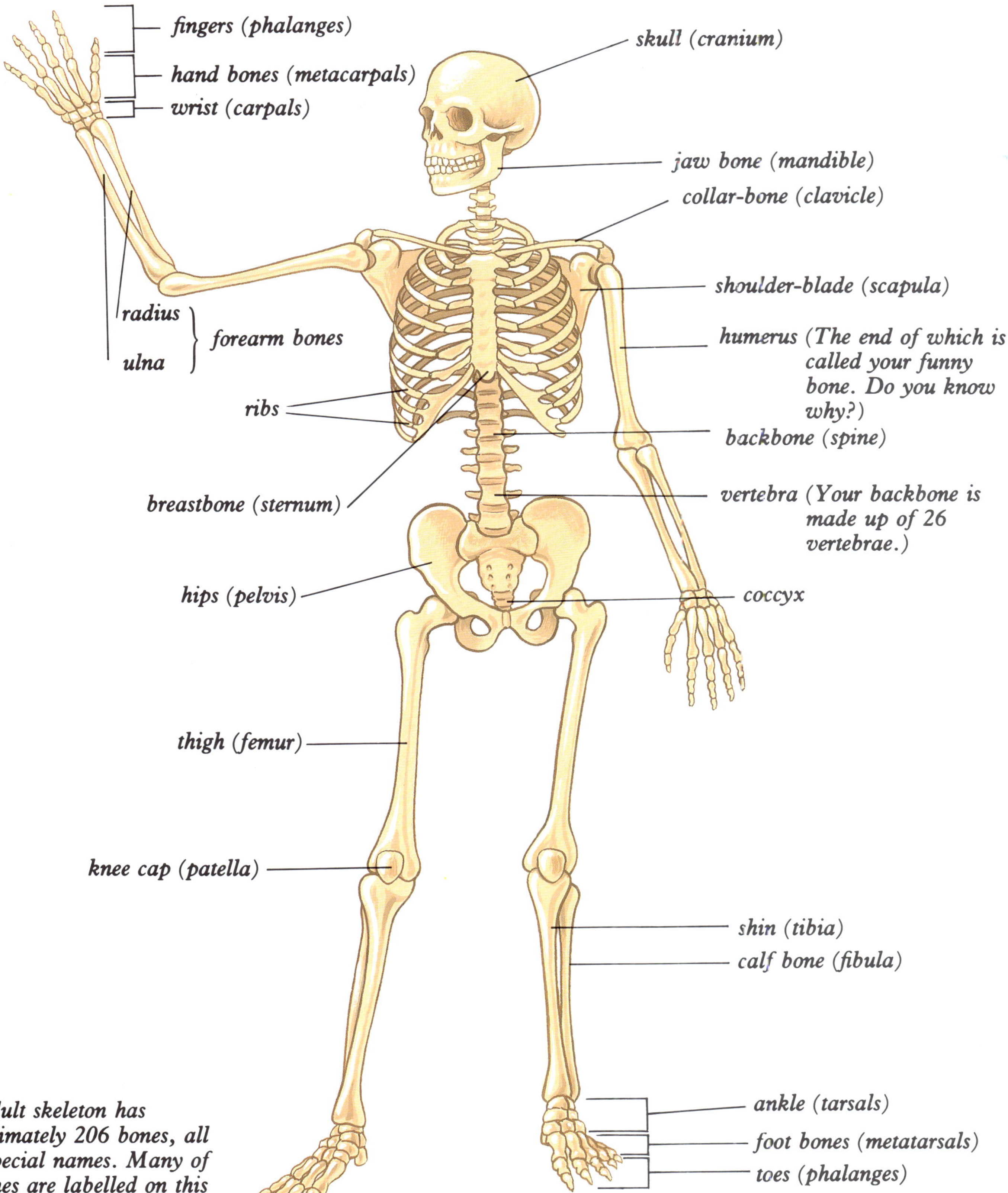

The adult skeleton has approximately 206 bones, all with special names. Many of the bones are labelled on this diagram of a skeleton. Some of these bones have more than one name.

What is bone?

Bone is an extremely strong, light material made of minerals and water. The inside of bone is living material and water.

How bones change

Our bones change as we grow older. A baby's skeleton starts to form seven months before birth, inside its mother. A newborn baby has soft, flexible and bendy bones. They are made of white, rubbery **cartilage**. Babies actually have more bones than adults. There are about 350 separate bones in an infant's skeleton. Over time, as a child grows, many of them join together to form larger bones.

Gradually, most of the cartilage turns into hard, non-living bone which surrounds the living material in the middle. As you grow older, more and more of the cartilage hardens in this way. Bands of cartilage are left at the ends of the bones and take much longer than the rest to harden. In some parts of the body, the cartilage never hardens. Feel your nose and ears. They are fairly stiff but still bendy. The cartilage in them never turns to bone.

Our bones change in other ways too. Run your finger up your shin bone. Can you feel any little bumps or nicks? Compare your leg with the leg of a very young child, aged under two. Notice how smooth their bones feel. Every time you fall over or bang into something, your bones get slightly chipped and dented — just like your bicycle when you're a little careless on it! Unlike a bicycle, the bone quickly heals itself but after every bruise you will notice a new little bump on the bone.

Growing up

Have you noticed how different parts of you seem to grow quite suddenly, in spurts? The sudden increase in height can happen from about the age of ten upwards. Girls usually start shooting up tall first but when boys follow a year or more later, most of them overtake the girls.

Growing up happens in a special order, starting with the head, hands and feet, then the arms and legs and finally the body. While some parts are waiting for the others to catch up, you may feel rather awkward and clumsy. You need plenty of exercise while you are growing fast, to build up muscle to match the new bone growth.

Some fish, including sharks, have no proper bones. Their 'skeleton' is made up of tough cartilage instead.

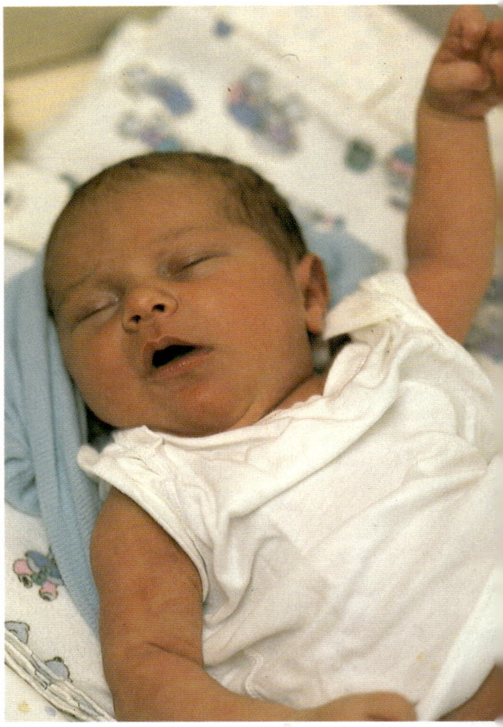

Babies have soft, flexible bones.

Old people often have thin, brittle bones.

Bone is constantly being broken down and re-built as old bone cells are exchanged for new ones. When you are young, your bones build up more than they break down and you grow bigger and stronger. Between the ages of about 25 and 35, the building-up and breaking-down processes are balanced. Then, as you get older, the breaking-down process very gradually takes over. In old age, the bones become thin and brittle and break easily.

Bones are built up, strengthened and repaired by the food that is in the blood which flows to them. Regular exercise is the best way to increase the flow of blood round your body and ensure that the food in it reaches the bones fast.

Beneath the sheath is a hard, solid outer layer of bone which surrounds lightweight material rather like honeycomb. Bundles of stringy fibres run through the bone to give it strength.

Journey into bone

Blood enters bone through a network of fine tubes called blood vessels. If you can look at a piece of cut bone from a butcher's shop, you should be able to see the holes which the blood vessels pass through.

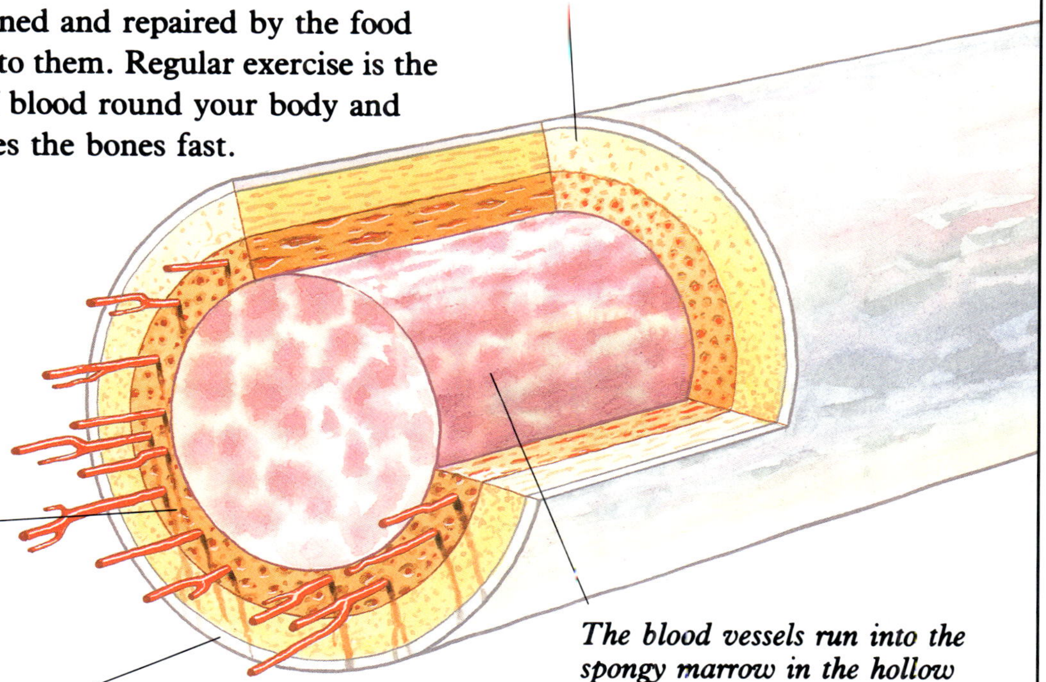

There is also a thin outer layer of blood vessels and special cells which repair damaged bone. All bones, except at the joints, are covered with this layer which is called the sheath.

The blood vessels run into the spongy marrow in the hollow centre of the bone. The marrow manufactures the important red cells that are in our blood.

Cells

All living things are made up of tiny packages called cells. These are the building bricks of which living things are made. The human body is made up of many millions of different kinds of cells — bone cells, muscle cells, skin cells, nerve cells, blood cells, etc. Simply, cells are made up of an outer wall with a jelly-like substance inside.

Many cells have the ability to divide and form new cells. It may help to think of a cell as a factory. Living cells need food as fuel and raw materials as well as oxygen to change the food into energy and materials to build new cells. Did you know that your skin is continuously wearing away and that you produce new skin cells all the time?

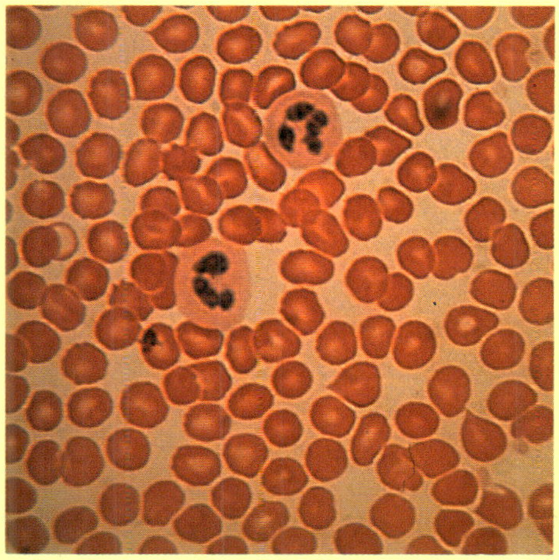

Human blood cells magnified 200 times

Joints

Do you know the song which goes, 'The knee bone's connected to the thigh bone, the thigh bone's connected to the hip bone . . .'? What an amazing piece of engineering the human skeleton is! The point where two bones are connected so that part of the body can move or bend is called a joint. Most joints allow movement in some directions but not others.

Tendons
The bones are pulled by flat, stretchy bands of muscle which are attached to the bones by springy ropes called tendons. These are even stronger than ligaments. They grow on to the bones.

Cartilage
At each joint, the two bone ends facing one another have a protective cap of cartilage which act as shock absorbers when you run or jump. They also help reduce friction between the two bones. However, this protection can be damaged if you fall or jump on something very hard and jar the bone ends together. Joggers who pound along hard roads protect the cartilage in their leg joints by wearing running shoes with good spongy soles.

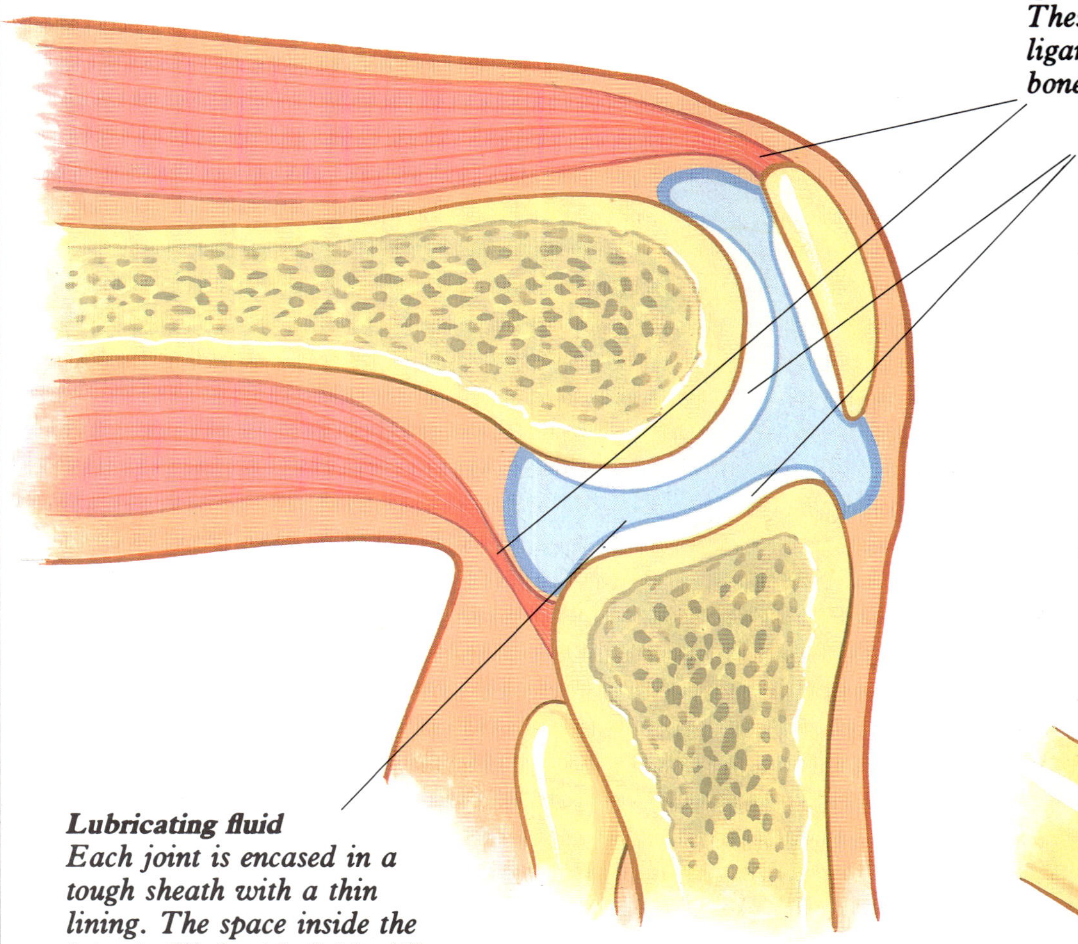

Lubricating fluid
Each joint is encased in a tough sheath with a thin lining. The space inside the joint is filled with fluid. All engineers know that moving parts need lubrication to keep them sliding over each other smoothly without roughness or friction which may cause them to wear out. Our joints need to be lubricated in the same way. The fluid in our joints moistens the muscles and tendons keeping them slippery so that they can move properly.

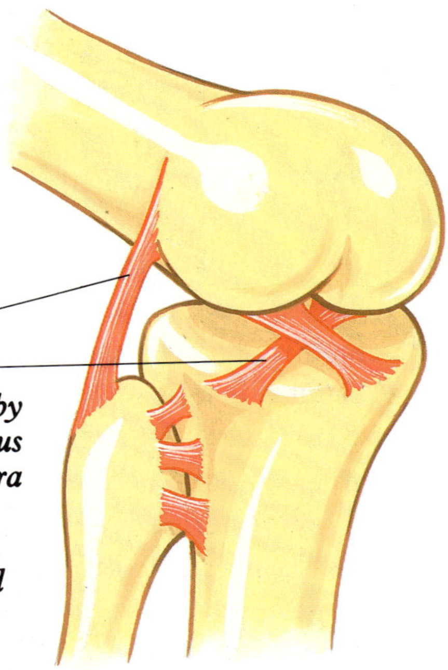

Ligaments
The joints are held together by tough strips of flexible, fibrous ligaments. They provide extra strength at the joint by strapping the bones together. They allow the joint to bend but prevent it from being pulled too far in the wrong direction.

When you throw a ball, each hinge joint in the arm unfolds in turn. There are three hinge joints in each finger. The wrist is a joint that has eight bones which allow it to rock and turn. The elbow is a huge joint which 'locks' the arm in a strong, straight line. The shoulder has a ball-and-socket joint which allows you to twist or swivel your arm.

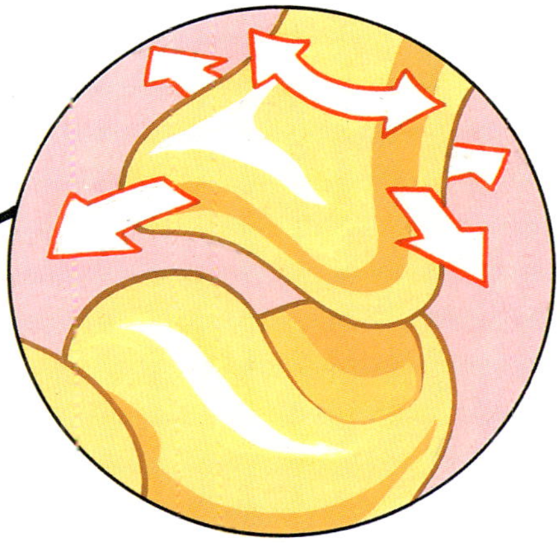

Saddle joint
There are saddle joints in our thumbs which allow movement in two directions. Humans are the only animals to have this especially useful movement.

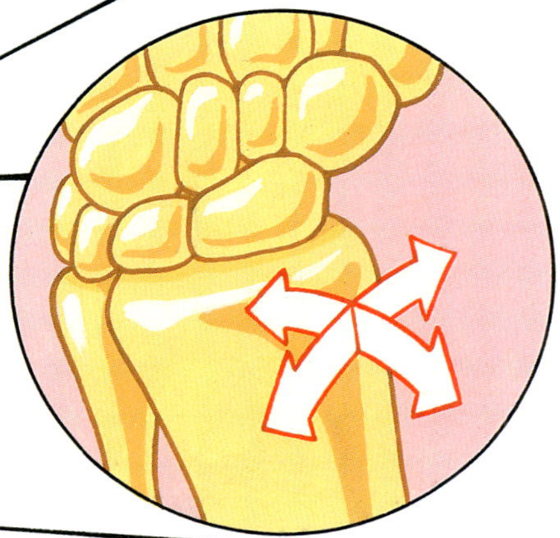

Wrist joint
The wrist bones of the hand fit into a hollow at the end of the arm bone. This allows the hand to move from side to side as well as forwards and backwards.

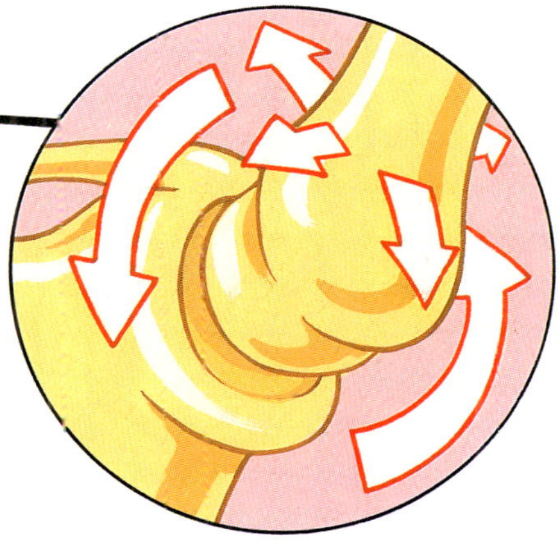

Ball-and-socket joint
The upper arm is connected to the shoulder by a ball-and-socket joint. The top of the arm bone has a ball-shaped end which fits snugly into a socket in the shoulder. This allows movement in any direction. Our thigh bones are connected to our hips by ball-and-socket joints too.

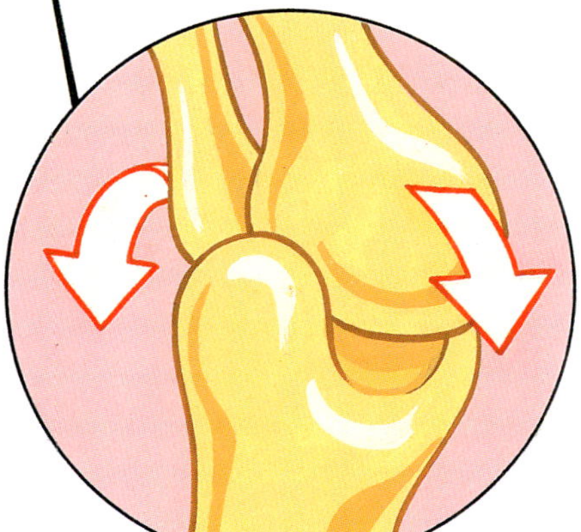

Hinge joint
Fingers, knees and elbows have hinge joints that only allow movement in one direction in the same way that the hinges on a door only allow it to open or close.

The human spine

Our spines are made up of 26 bones, each one with a hole through it. The bones line up like a long tunnel and protect a delicate bundle of nerves called the spinal cord which is vital to almost all our movements.

The 26 bones in the spine are called vertebrae. Between each bone is a springy disc of cartilage. These discs allow the bones to slide over each other a little way so that the spine can bend. They also allow the spine to twist a little. If you watch someone flexing their spine, you should be able to see each of the vertebrae moving.

At the top of the spine there is a special pivot joint. This allows your head to turn around almost completely. Another special joint between the top vertebra and the skull gives the head a wide range of movement so that it can tip backwards, forwards and sideways at several different angles.

The human spine is very uniform in length. Among Europeans, it varies only between 72 and 78 cm on average. The difference in people's height is mainly due to variations in leg lengths.

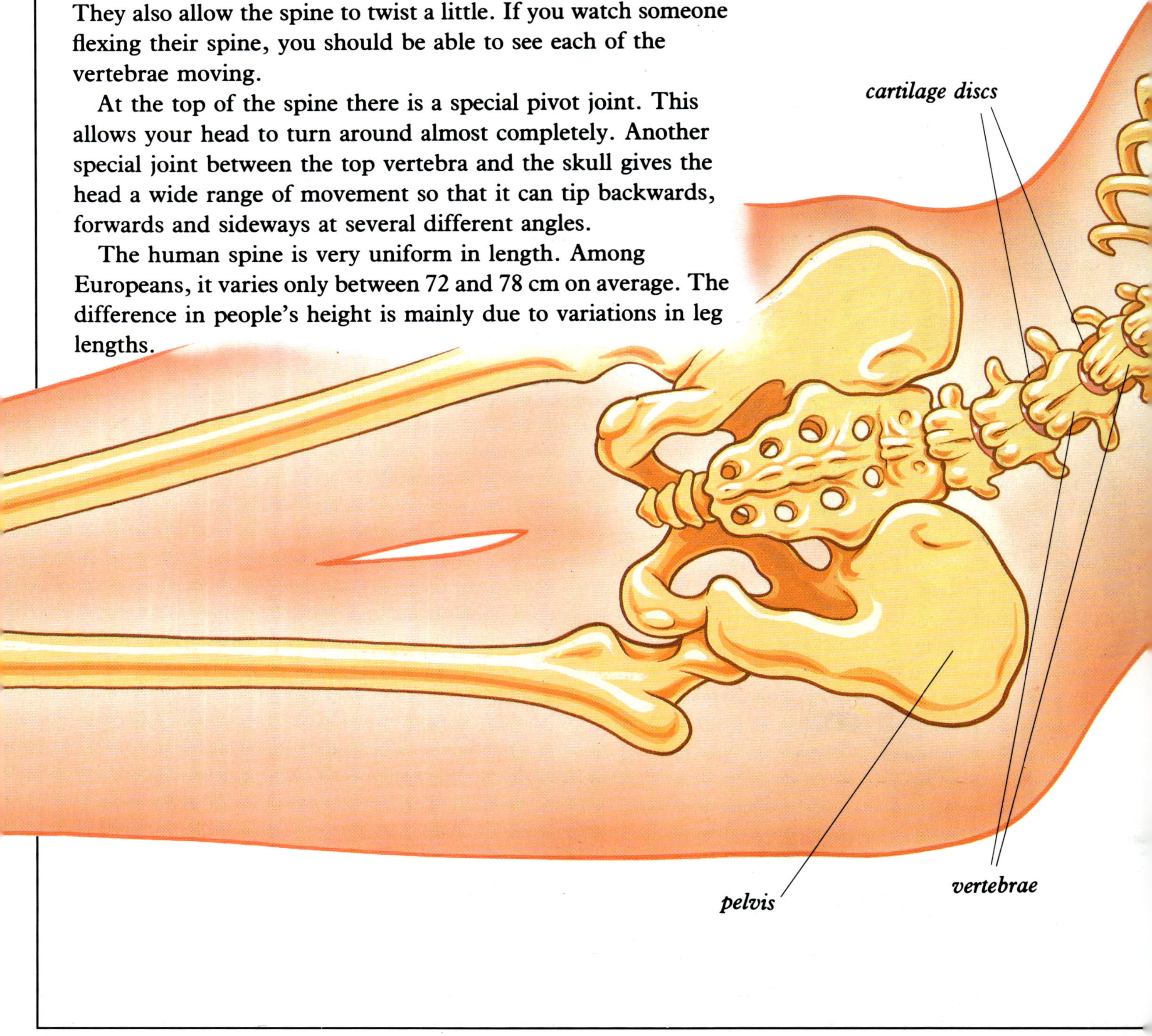

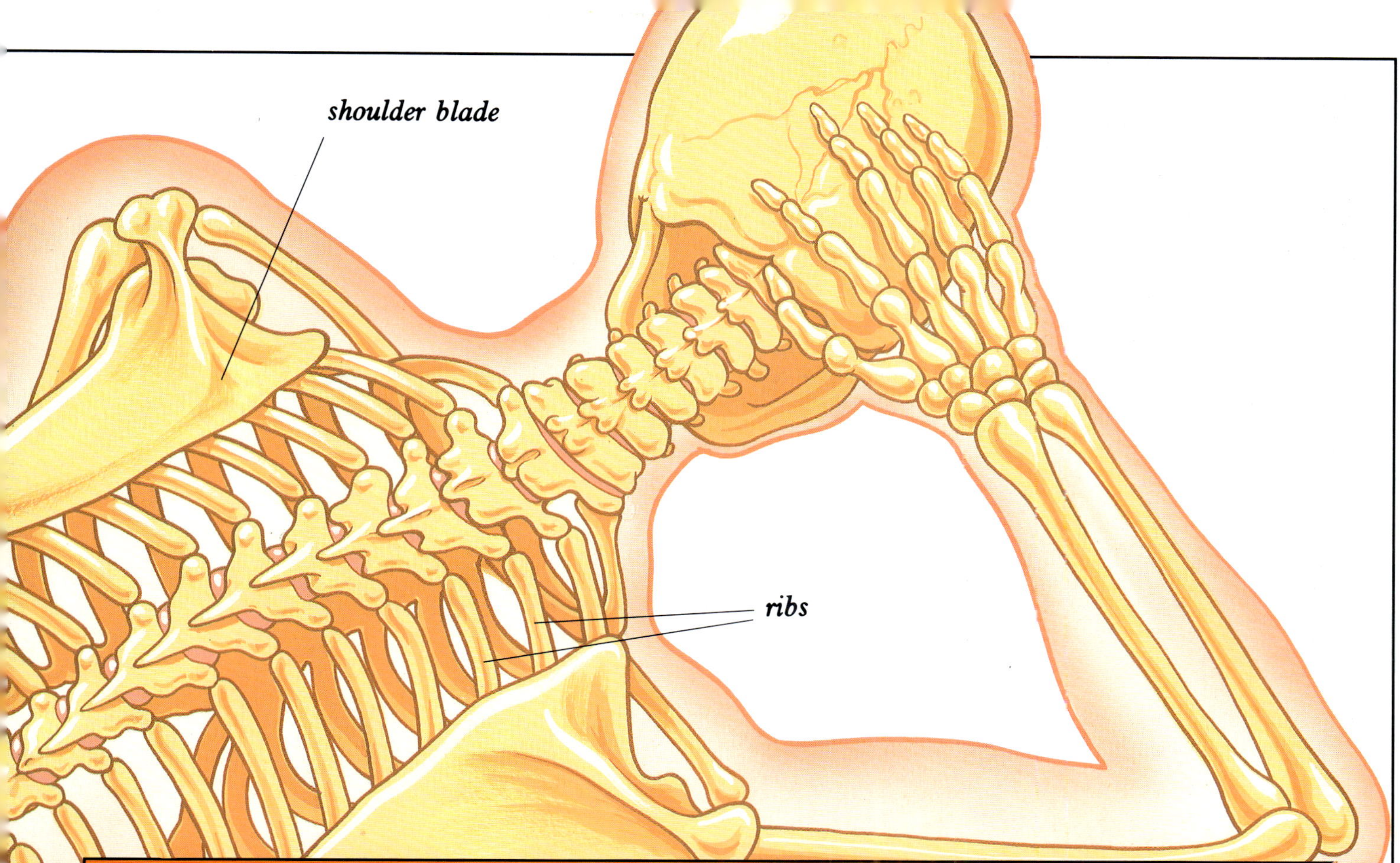

Every mammal you will ever see has just seven vertebrae in its neck. That's right! You have seven, a tiny mouse has seven, the long necked giraffe has seven, a dog has seven, a cat has seven, a chimp has seven . . .

Making model joints

Hinge joints

Each of your arms has a hinge joint at the elbow. The hinge lets your forearm move up and down.

You can model this hinge joint in all sorts of ways. Here are a few ideas. Can you think of others?

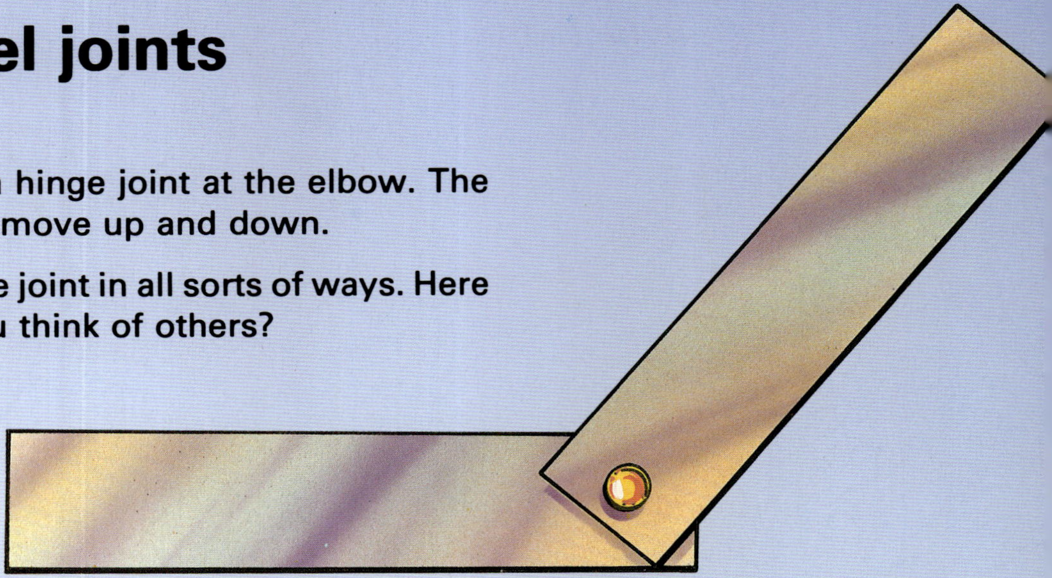

cardboard strips and a paper-fastener

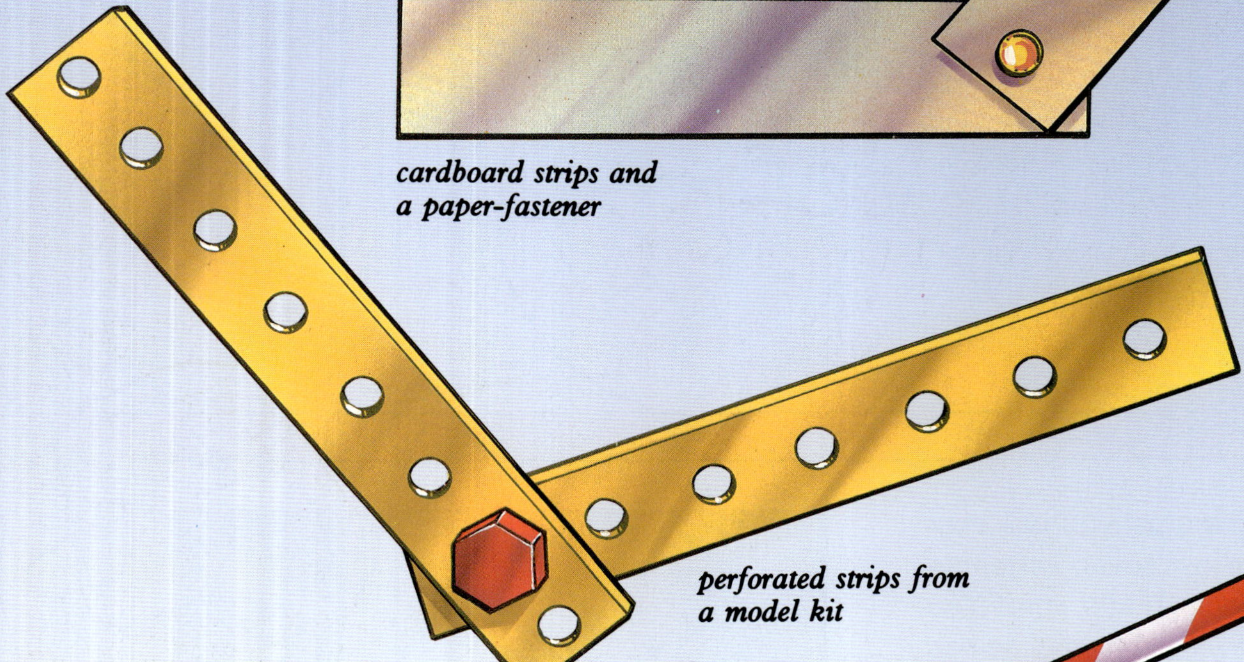

perforated strips from a model kit

straws and a pipe-cleaner

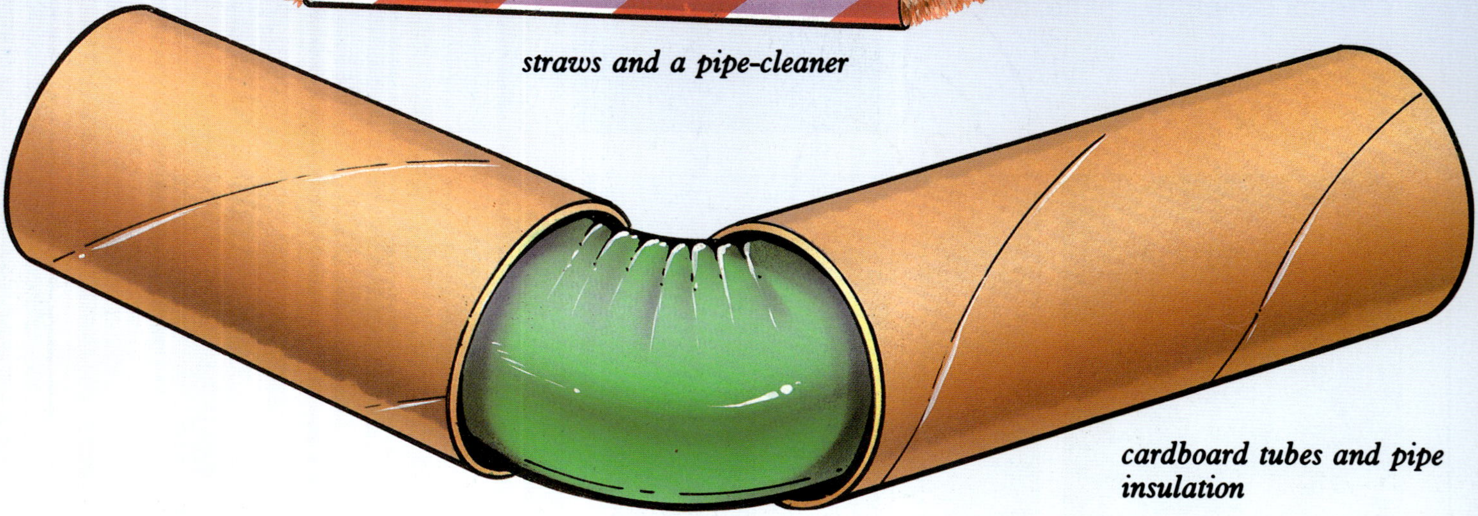

cardboard tubes and pipe insulation

Why aren't these model arms like your own arms?

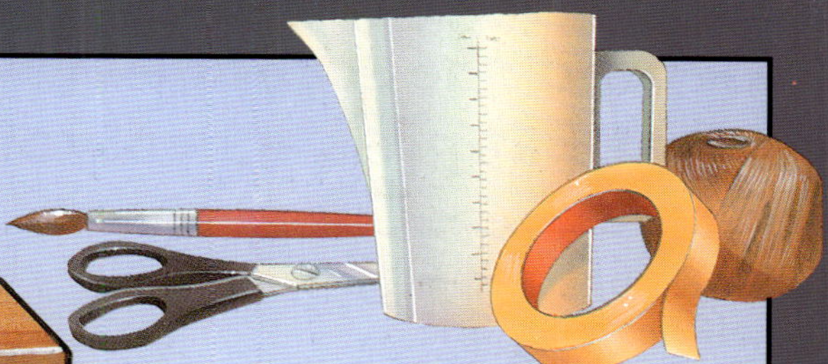

If you cut the ends of two pieces of thin wood at an angle like this –

– you will make a joint that will only bend one way, just like your arm.

Ball-and-socket joints

Your shoulder joints are ball-and-socket joints. Your arm can move round in a circle to bowl a ball or serve at tennis. Ball-and-socket joints are harder to model than hinge joints. Here are two ways — can you think of any others?

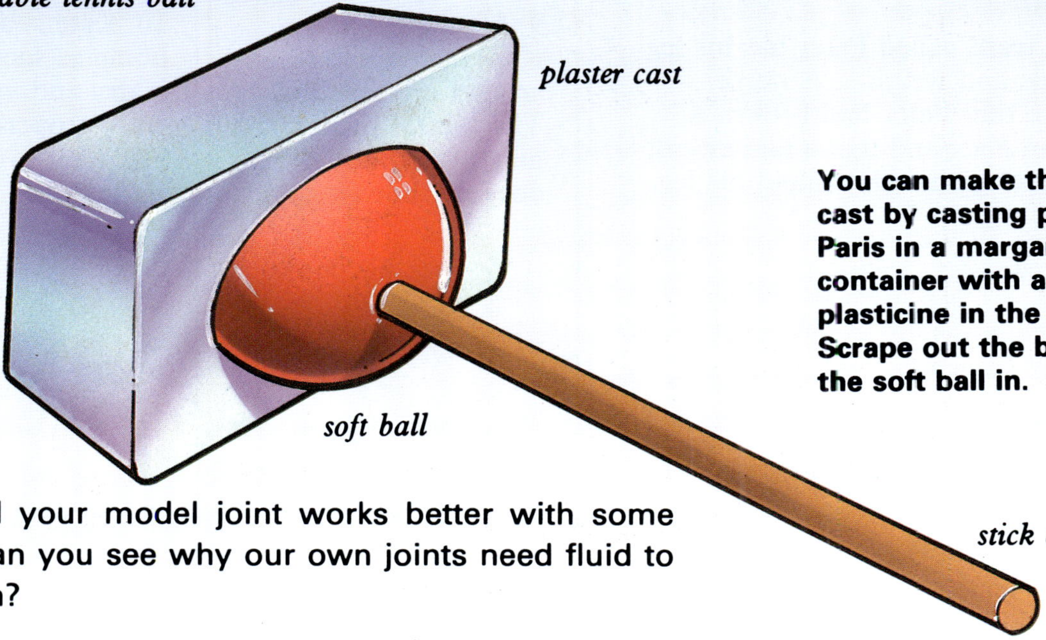

You can make the plaster cast by casting plaster of Paris in a margarine container with a ball of plasticine in the centre. Scrape out the ball and fit the soft ball in.

You may find your model joint works better with some lubrication. Can you see why our own joints need fluid to lubricate them?

Behind the scenes — what happens when you break a bone?

1 Kate has just fallen off her bike. She can't move her leg. A man who saw what happened has called an ambulance.

2 The ambulance attendants put Kate's leg in a splint which is made of strong plastic blown up with air like a lilo. This is to hold the bone still. They carry her into the ambulance on a stretcher and take her to the nearest hospital.

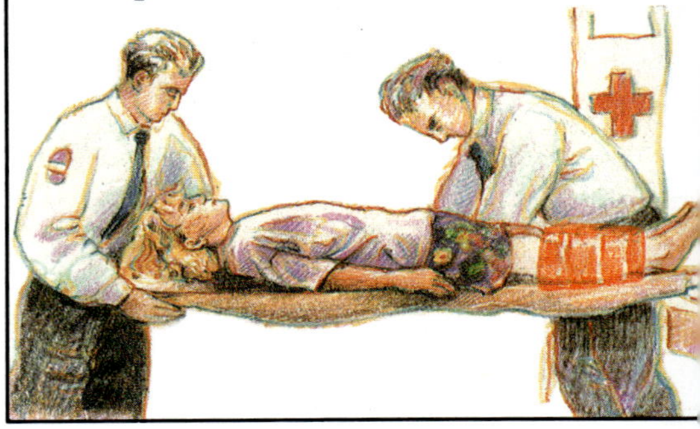

4 The doctor tells Kate that she will go next to the X-ray department to have a photograph taken of the broken bone. The X-ray shows that she needs to have an operation to mend it.

5 Kate is taken to a bed in the children's ward. The nurses make her comfortable and Kate's mum sits with her and reads her a story.

6 When it is time for her operation, Kate is taken o her bed to the operating theatre. One doctor gives her an injection in her arm and Kate falls fast asleep Then the doctors pull on Kate's leg to make the broken bone straight. Because Kate is asleep, she doesn't feel anything.

8 A boy in the ward called Peter has his leg held up by cords and weights. A nurse explains to Kate that Peter had broken a bigger bone than Kate and that a plaster cast would not be strong enough to hold his leg while it is mending.

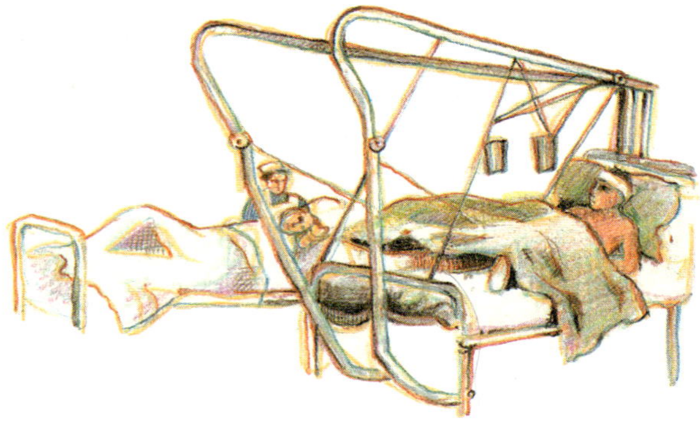

9 After a few days, Kate learns to hop around on crutches. The plaster makes her leg itch but it does not hurt.

10 Kate is allowed to go home as soon as her plaster is dry and when she can walk properly with crutches Peter has to stay in hospital until his leg is mended.

3 At the Accident and Emergency Department of the hospital, Kate is given an injection to stop her leg hurting. The nurses gently remove the splint so that the doctor can examine her leg. She says that Kate's leg may be broken. They put her leg into another splint to hold it still.

7 Then the doctors put a plaster bandage on her leg which will go hard and hold the leg straight and still. When Kate wakes up she is back in the ward with her leg in the plaster cast.

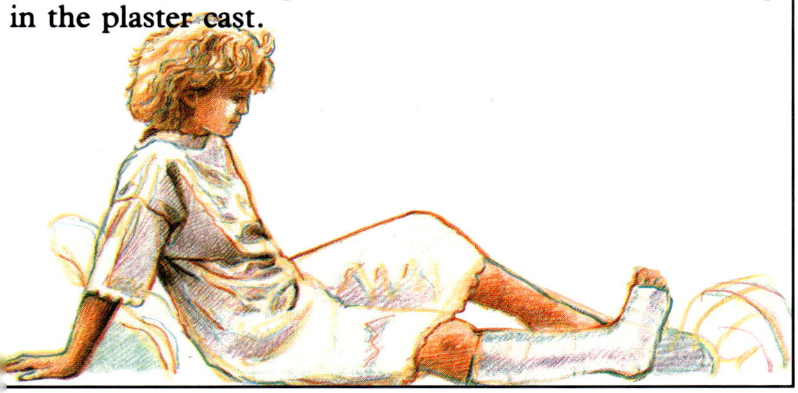

11 A few weeks later, Kate has a final X-ray taken to check that the bone has completely mended. The plaster is taken off. She will soon be running and walking normally again.

Know your fractures

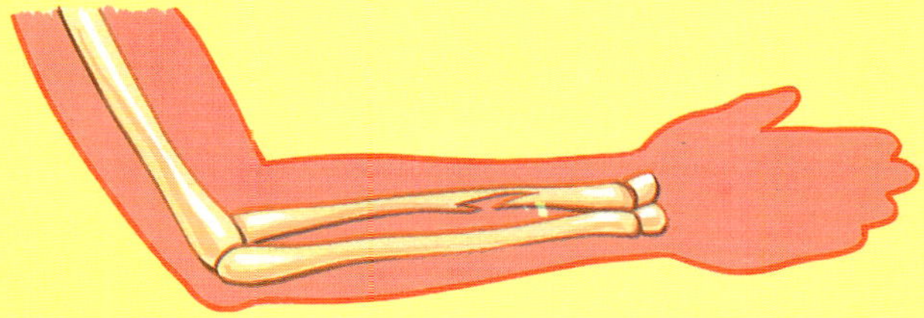

Greenstick fracture
The bone is only partly broken or bent.

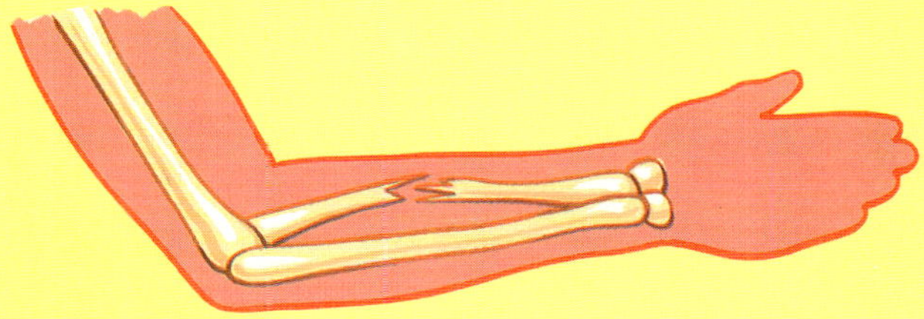

Closed fracture
The bone breaks completely but does not come through the skin.

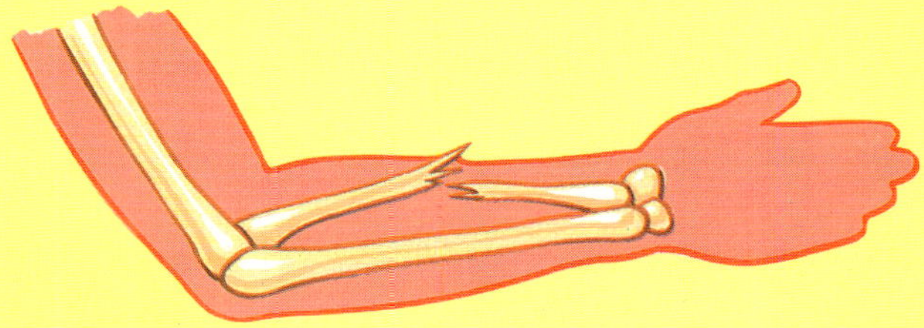

Compound fracture
The broken bone breaks through the skin making an open wound which may become infected.

How a bone mends

When a bone breaks, blood vessels lying along the fracture line are torn. Blood seeps out and forms a **clot** between the pieces of broken bone. Soon, new blood vessels and bone-forming cells begin to make new material. This new material forms a bridge between the pieces of broken bone. After about six to twelve weeks, the new bone is much stronger and ready to move again. The older you get, however, the longer it takes for bones to mend.

Muscle movements

Can you feel your muscles? Hold your bare arm out straight, sideways. Then raise your hand and forearm. Does a bulge appear on your arm halfway between your shoulder and elbow? That's muscle!

Muscles enable you to move. Every movement you make depends on muscles. There are over 600 in your body, ranging from the tiny one that moves your smallest bone which is in your ear to the large, strong muscles in your legs and bottom. A muscle is made up of a bunch of tiny fibres. The bones of our skeleton act as a framework for the muscles to pull against. The muscles are attached to the bones by bands of strong, fibrous material called tendons.

Muscles vary in shape. Those attached to bones are usually a tapered sausage shape. Others are like ribbons, while in the arm and shoulder, there are fan-shaped muscles that raise the arm outwards or pull it down to the side.

There are two types of muscle:

- Those that we use when we decide to make a movement such as standing up, walking or putting a hand up. These are called voluntary muscles.
- Those that move automatically so that we do not have to think about them to make them work. These muscles operate the vital organs such as our lungs and our digestive system. They work all the time, even when we are asleep. These are called involuntary muscles. The muscle in the heart which is called cardiac muscle is a type of involuntary muscle which works automatically, day and night.

How do voluntary muscles move?

Voluntary muscles always work in pairs. As one muscle or group of muscles **contracts** to move a bone, its paired muscle or group of muscles relaxes and becomes longer to allow the movement to take place. There are similar sets of muscles on each side of the body.

When a muscle contracts, its fibres are shortened making them thicker. This is what is happening when you see the bulge appearing in your arm. At the same time, the fibres in the paired muscle get longer as they relax. Feel your arm muscles again and move your forearm up and down. Can you feel the muscles contracting and relaxing in turn?

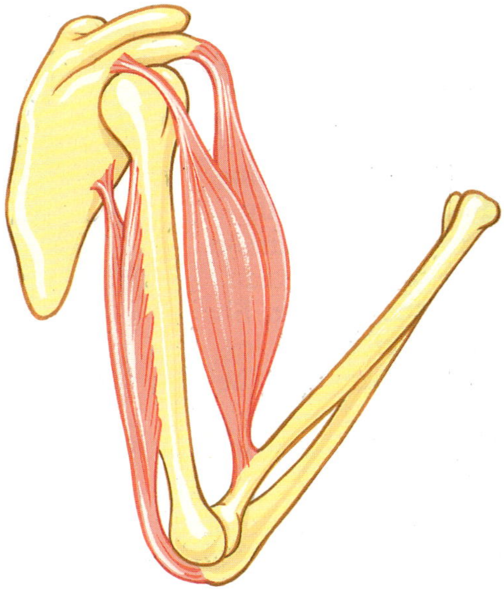

Bent arm – *biceps muscle tensed, triceps muscle relaxed*

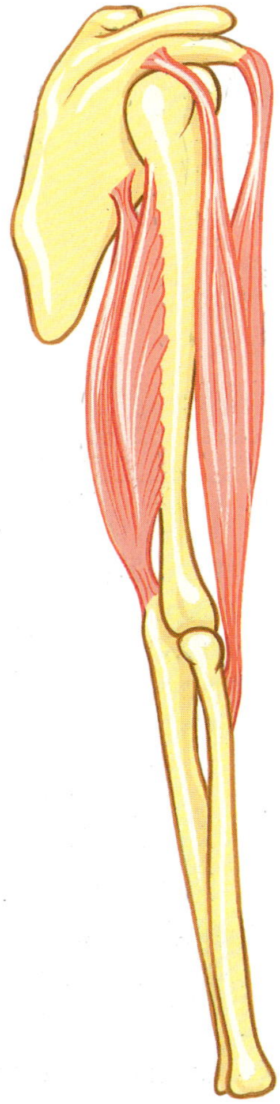

Straight arm – *biceps muscle relaxed, triceps muscle tensed*

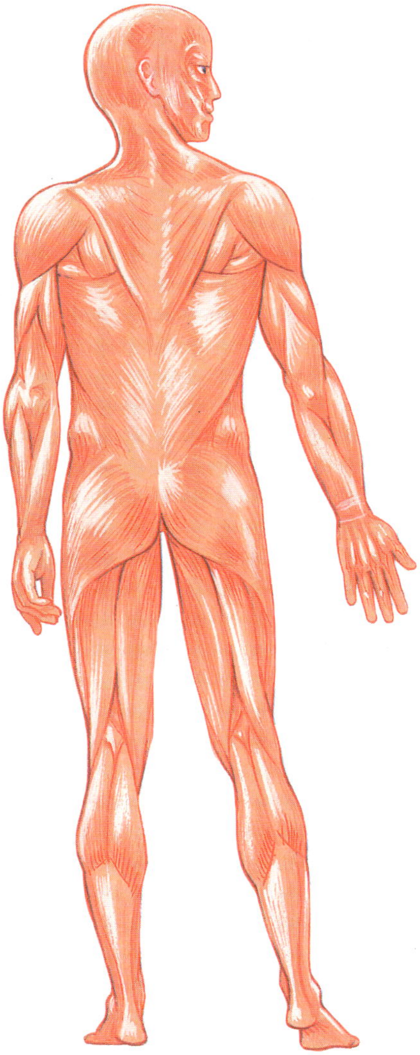

Diagram showing the muscles of the body

When you bend your arm, your biceps muscle contracts and your triceps muscle lengthens. When you straighten the arm again, your triceps muscle contracts to pull the relaxed biceps muscle back to its longer shape.

Voluntary muscles know when to move because they receive messages from the brain through the nerves they are attached to. When you decide to do something, like throwing a ball, your brain (which is your control centre) sends a signal to the nerves which puts them into action to tell the right muscles to work. You will probably not be aware that you have made a decision to move muscles when you are doing something familiar like walking or blinking because you are so used to doing it.

How do involuntary muscles move?

The nerves which send messages to involuntary muscles run automatically.

Like voluntary muscles, involuntary muscles produce movement by contracting and relaxing. They are specialized to produce the long, slow contractions needed to work the major organs. Rings of muscles in our intestines tighten and relax in waves which push the food and fibre along. And, of course, the heart muscle keeps beating regularly to pump blood round the body. There are also some much less obvious involuntary muscles, for instance, the tiny muscles which make the hair on our skin stand on end and give us goose-pimples or those in the iris which make the pupil in the eye bigger or smaller.

Modelling your muscles

You can see how your arm muscles work by using the model arm that you made from thin wood on page 13.

- Attach two elastic bands to represent the arm muscles. Fix them on to the straight arm with drawing-pins. Try them in different places until they work really well.

By adding a hand made from stiff card, can you:

- make a model that waves?
- make a model that will lift a plastic cup?

Muscle strength

Push and pull

We need strong muscles to lift and carry. Our arms are strong. Try lifting a weight like a large book with one arm. Put it on the palm of your hand. Roll your sleeve right up while you do it so that you can watch your arm. Can you see and feel the muscles hardening? Which muscles are working? Now lay your arm on the table with the palm of your hand facing up. Push down. Watch your arm again. Which muscles are working now?

Which muscles were bigger — the lifting muscles or the pushing down muscles? Can you see why you might twist your arm round to push downwards to put in a rounders stump, for example?

When you use your muscles, you use up energy which you need to replace. You can replace it by eating food and breathing in fresh air. Your body needs oxygen from the air to 'burn up' your food.

Take plenty of exercise too. Your body needs constant practice at keeping the muscles working well.

Your muscles can lift amazing weights when they are tensed up. Try this party trick. With three friends, stand round another friend who is sitting on a chair. All press down firmly (not hard!) on the seated person's head and shoulders. Press for a few seconds. Then all together and very quickly, slip your hands underneath your friend and lift a few centimetres. You'll be surprised how easy it is.

The work and exercise you do builds up, or develops, your muscles. People in different jobs develop different muscles. How do you think a carpenter's muscles would differ from a hairdresser's?

Measure your muscle strength

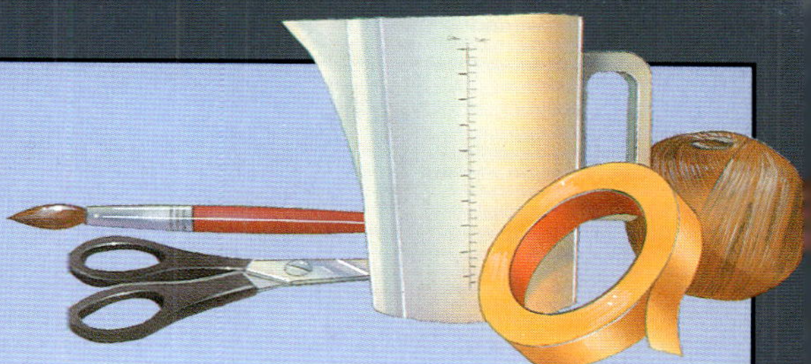

You can measure the strength of your muscles. Here are some suggestions. Try them and develop some other ways for yourself. Make sure your ideas are safe and don't strain yourself. It's no good proving you're the strongest if you end up hurting yourself!

Leg strength

- Test your leg strength by lying down and pressing against some bathroom scales held against a wall.

(Why press against the wall? Why not stand on the scales? What would you be measuring then?)

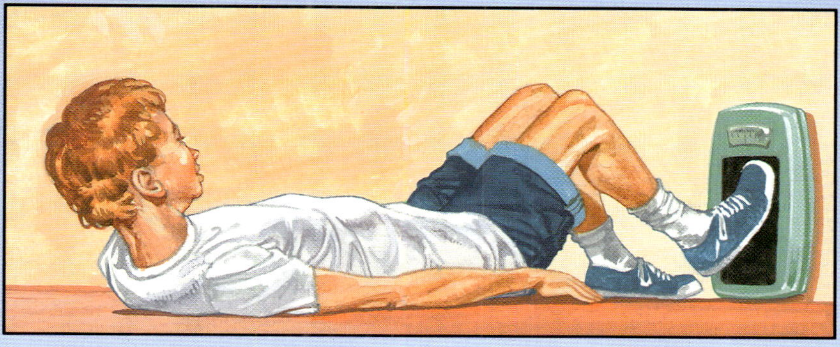

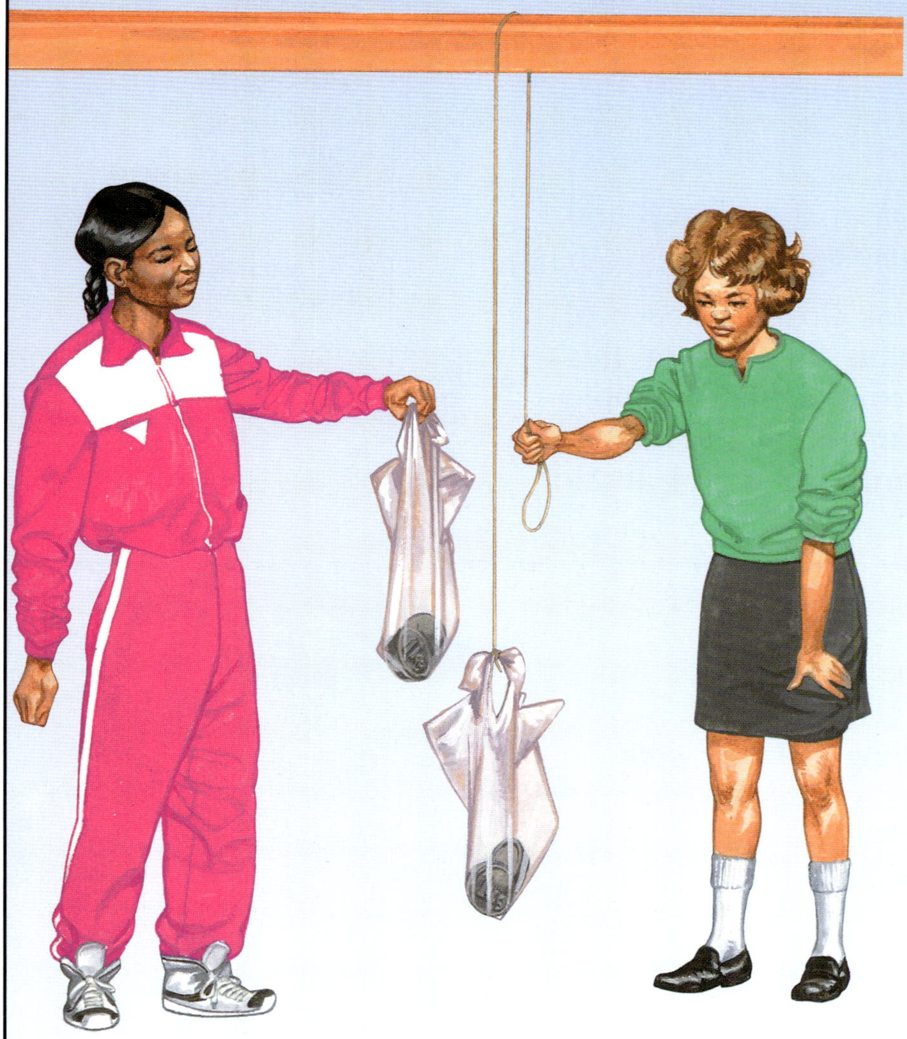

Lifting strength of your arm

- With your arm stretched out at full length in front of you, try lifting a carrier bag with weights in it. How much can you lift keeping your arm stretched out straight and without straining? (You could hang the carrier bag on a spring balance so that you can measure the weight more quickly.)

Pulling strength of your arm

Now see how well you can pull down.

- Attach a strong spring balance to a secure point or put a strong rope over a beam or bar of the PE apparatus and tie the other end to the handles of a carrier bag with weights in it.
- Pull firmly down with your palm facing downwards and your arm stretched out straight. How much can you pull without putting your weight on it and without straining?

All systems go!

It takes the brain, the amazing organ in your head which controls everything that happens in your body, and your complicated system of muscles, joints and nerves to re-position each of your bones every time you move. There are particular sets of muscles and bones which are designed to make particular movements.

What goes into a simple movement?

You may find it easy to pick up a book, but many people find even a simple movement like that quite difficult — people with muscular diseases or **arthritis,** for example. The fact is that picking up a book is actually a very complex thing to do. It involves muscles, bones, the senses of touch and sight, nerves and the brain all acting together. And that's not counting the other body systems — **respiration, digestion** and blood without which none of these could operate at all!

- Pick up a book in slow motion.
- Watch carefully. What happens to the bones and joints? What happens to the muscles?
- Follow this flow diagram and look closely at each of the stages that make it possible to perform this simple movement. Work in a group of three people to do this — one to do the movement, one to look at the bone and joint movements and one to look at the muscles and their movements.

1 *Eyes and brain see book and judge distance.*

4 *Eyes and brain continue to judge distance. Fingers begin to uncurl.*

Man carrying bale

The tough hand closes gently on the load;
  Out of the mind, a voice
Calls 'Lift!' and the arms, remembering well their work,
  Lengthen and pause for help.
Then a slow ripple flows along the body,
While all the muscles call to one another:
  'Lift!' and the bulging bale
  Floats like a butterfly in June.

Harold Monro

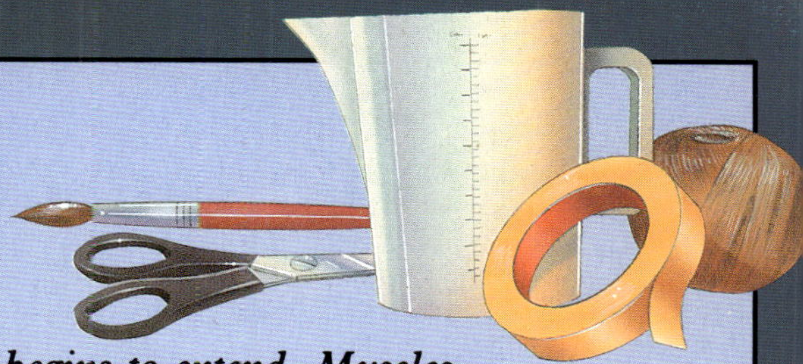

2 *Brain communicates message to arm and hands.*

3 *Arm begins to extend. Muscles and arm joints work. Body bends forward.*

5 *Arm is extended. Fingers curl around book.*

6 *Fingers grip book. Arm begins to raise. Muscles take strain. Brain processes information.*

- Now choose your own very simple action. Look at what happens as one of you carries out the action. Which bones, joints and muscles move?
- Draw a step-by-step flow diagram like the one here to show what happens in the action you have chosen. Write what is happening in each box.
- Read your diagram to your group or class. Can they guess what is happening?
- When they have guessed correctly, demonstrate the movement to the class while giving a commentary. One of you could describe how the bones and joints move and another, the muscle movements.

Incredible muscles

Athletes and sports players spend hours training and strengthening their muscles. For some events, particular muscles have to be developed even more than the rest. A tennis player, for example, needs particularly strong muscles in one arm. If you observe a good tennis player, you will probably notice that the muscles in the arm used to serve and play all the shots are bigger than the muscles in the other arm.

The Russian heavyweight weightlifting champion, Vasili Alexeyev, developed his chest muscles so much that his chest measured 156.6 cm when he weighed his most at 158.7 kg. Measure your own chest — how does it compare with Vasili's?

Weightlifters increase the thickness of their muscle fibres during training. They learn to use more fibres at one time to give them extra strength. Most people don't use all the fibres in a muscle when they make an action. Some of the fibres are kept for emergencies. This is why some people in emergency situations have been able to lift incredible weights which they could not normally manage.

Vasili Alexeyev

The biggest of the muscles in your body is the buttock muscle which moves the longest bone in your body, the thigh bone. You can exercise your buttock muscle at any time, even when you're sitting down. Just keep squeezing your bottom hard, then relaxing it.

Carl Lewis

Kangaroos have long, thin, powerful back legs for jumping. The top speed ever recorded by a kangaroo was 64 kph and the longest jump was 13.5 m. Compare that with record achievements by humans. Top sprinters like Carl Lewis have had maximum speeds of about 40 kph recorded. The long jump record was held for almost 23 years by the American, Bob Beamon, who jumped 8.9 m in the 1968 Olympic Games in Mexico City.

Bob Beamon

The longest known jump by a frog was by Santjie, a female South African sharp-nosed frog which jumped 10.3 m in a competition in 1977. These creatures' bodies can cope with such enormous jumps because they have tremendously powerful leg muscles for their size.

Heartbeat

The most important muscle in your body is the heart. It pumps blood containing oxygen around the body which supplies all your bones and tissues with food to keep them working and renew their cells. Your heart works automatically every day and night of your life.

Ask a friend if you can listen to his heart. If you put your ear next to his chest, you should be able to hear a soft, regular noise, rather like a drum beating. We say that our heart 'beats'. Doctors use a stethoscope which makes this 'lubb-dubb' sound louder so that they can hear it clearly. But what is it that actually makes this beating sound?

The heart is made up of four **chambers**, each one with muscular walls. About once a second, these walls contract and squeeze blood along strong tubes called arteries. The blood is pushed through a **non-return valve** on the right side of the heart into the artery which leads to the lungs. This valve makes sure the blood keeps flowing in the right direction. In the lungs, the blood gets rid of most of the carbon dioxide dissolved in it and collects fresh oxygen from the fresh air breathed in.

This blood then flows back into the left side of the heart and the next heart beat sends it out through another valve and into the artery system which runs all over the body. As the blood travels through the body, it delivers all its oxygen to the muscles and organs in the body.

You may have guessed by now that the sound you can hear when the heart beats is the sound produced by all the valves closing. These valves close very quickly to stop the blood going back where it's already been.

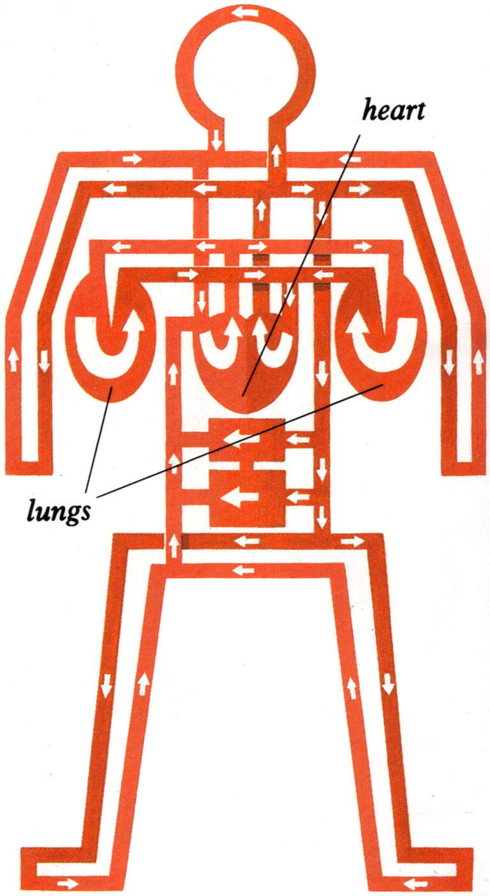

Diagram showing the circulation of blood in the body

Stethoscopes

Has a doctor ever listened to your chest? She may have used a stethoscope to listen to your breathing or your heart beating. A stethoscope cuts out all the other sounds around.

Try making a stethoscope.

- Use a cardboard tube or a length of plastic tube like hose-pipe to listen to your partner's heart.
- What happens if you add a plastic funnel to the end so that you listen to a greater body area? (You can make a funnel from the top of a washing-up bottle or by using a yoghurt pot with a hole in the bottom.)
- Do you find that you cover your other ear? Why?
- Can you hear your partner's heart? Can you hear her lungs? Can you hear her stomach churning?

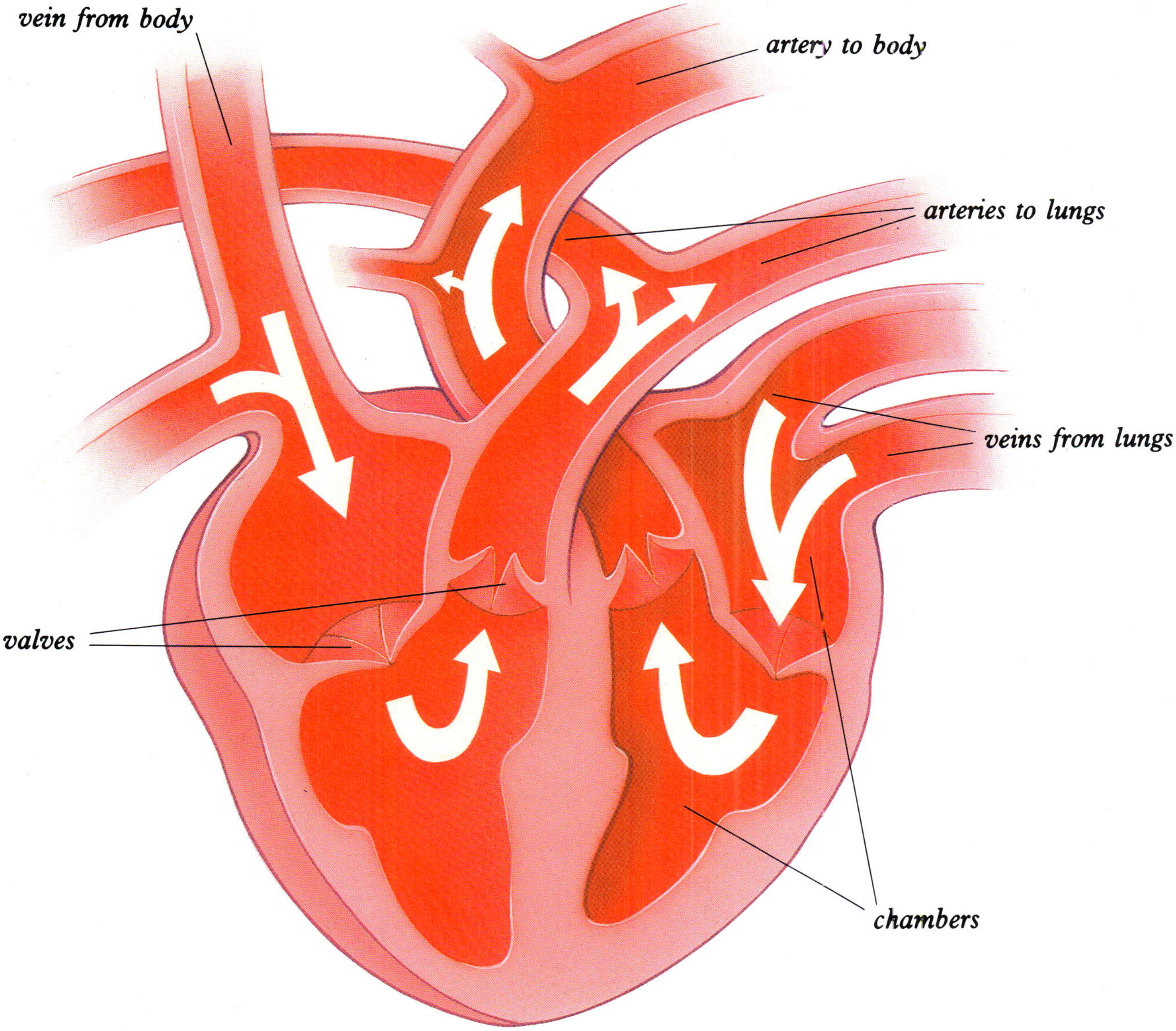

Cross-section through the heart

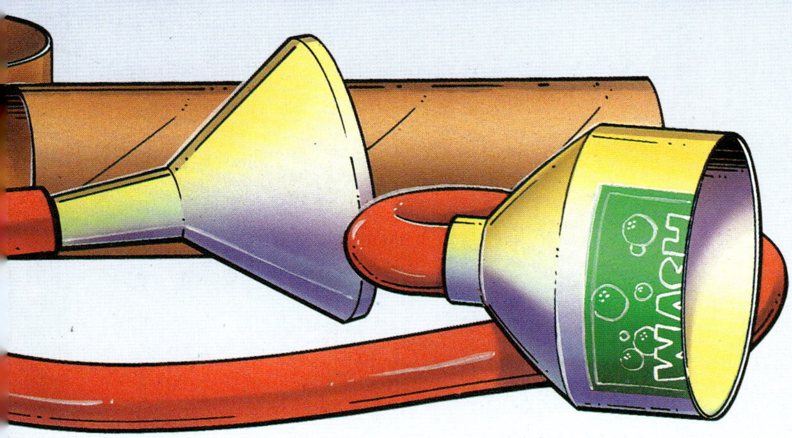

- Try listening to quiet sounds – put the stethoscope to a piece of rough paper as a worm moves across it. Can you hear the rasp of its bristles on the paper? (Remember to put the worm back carefully where you found it afterwards.)

Now try using a real stethoscope if possible.

Taking your pulse

Your heart beats faster when you are excited, frightened or energetic. When you move, your muscles need more oxygen to give the muscles energy. Your heart beats faster to increase the blood flow so that the extra oxygen required can reach the muscles. If someone is used to taking a lot of exercise and so is fit, his heart can speed up fast. An unfit person gets breathless and dizzy and begins to feel weak because he cannot get enough oxygen. As soon as you stop exercising, your pulse rate goes down. The fitter you are, the quicker it returns to normal.

We should exercise our bodies regularly. The heart needs to be exercised just like any other muscle. But sudden bursts of energy, or severe shocks, are bad for the heart. This is why it is important to do warm-up exercises before any energetic activity to allow the heart to speed up gently. A cooling down routine is important too so that the heart slows down gently.

Measure your pulse rate

Have you ever heard people talking about their pulse rate? When all the blood is pushed out of the heart, it surges through your arteries. Each surge is called a pulse. One of the best places to feel your pulse is on your wrist. Each time you feel your pulse, your heart is beating. Here are two ways of finding your pulse on your wrist:

- Sit still for a few minutes, then press two fingers firmly in the hollow along the outer bone of your wrist.
- Cut a piece of drinking straw about 2 cm long. Put one end over a drawing-pin. Place the upturned drawing-pin and straw on your wrist and watch it move up and down.

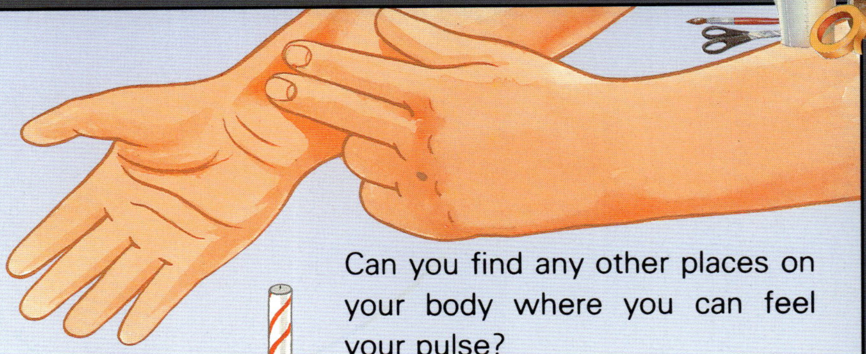

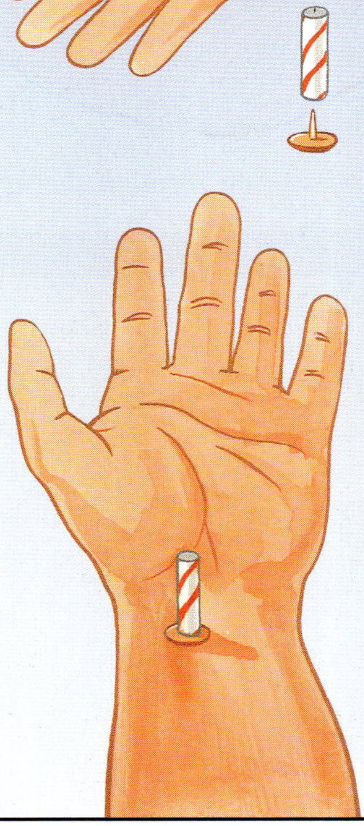

Can you find any other places on your body where you can feel your pulse?

- Use a stopwatch or clock to count how many times your pulse beats in one minute.
- Compare your pulse rate with your friends'. Make a chart to record the pulse rates of everyone in the class. Who has got the fastest and slowest pulse rates?
- Try comparing pulse rates again just after you've done some exercise. You could do it during a PE lesson. How do pulse rates change after exercise?

One Tuesday When I Was About Ten

One Tuesday when I was about ten
I swam thirty-two lengths
which is one mile
and when I climbed out of the water
I felt like a big fat lump of jelly
and my legs were made of rubber
and there was this huge man there
with tremendous muscles all over him
and I went up to him and I said,
'I've just swum a mile.'
And he said,
'How many lengths was that, then?'
'Thirty-two' I said,
and the man looked into the water and said,
'I've got a lad here who can do ninety.'

Michael Rosen

Let you body go

Me say get you bones movin, let you body go.
Get you heart beating, speed up no go slow.

Stick out you toes
feel you blood flows

Stretch you lickle leg
hang it on a peg — aya

Bend you in the middle
it no such a fiddle — bim

Straighten out you back
Fe no saggin like a sack

Twist you floppy neck — gribbit
say man what the heck

Stickle out you tongue
Then you song is sung

Me say get you bones movin, let you body go.
Get you heart beating, speed up no go slow.

John Rice

Look after your body

Take some exercise

Without exercise, your body and bones lose their strength, and spare energy from your food is stored as fat instead of being burnt up by your muscles. The extra weight and weakness make it even harder for your body to regain its fitness. Lack of exercise, for example when someone has a long stay in bed during illness, can lead to weaker bones.

Hard exercise, like cycling or swimming, is also helpful because it makes the blood flow faster round the body and increases the blood supply to the bones and muscles.

Regular exercise is the key to good health, strong bones and firm muscles. Exercise helps your mind as well as your body, making it easier for you to relax, feel happier and more energetic. But take care because many exercise fanatics overdo it and cause themselves more harm than good. Overworked muscles can make you feel exhausted. They need rest and massage to revive them. Strains and tears in ligaments and tendons cause painful swellings which need cold compresses and supporting bandages. Cramp is one of the most common complaints when people try an exercise they are not used to. It is a tightening up of the muscle and can be very painful. The best way to stop cramp continuing is to gently stretch out the muscle concerned and rub it hard.

Cycling is a good way to exercise

Marathon runners can often suffer from cramp

Boys playing football

Do you or any of your friends play sport regularly? Are there any footballers, dancers, swimmers, gymnasts or similar in the class? What exercise routines do they do to practise and improve their performance? How do they warm up?

Keep fit in space

Some of the first astronauts complained that their bodies felt weak when they returned to Earth. Scientists noticed that their bodies had lost some of the important calcium which normally helps keep bones strong. They discovered that because the astronauts had been weightless for most of their time in space, their bodies had no weight to push against. Their bodies became so light that their bones began to lose calcium. Once the astronauts had been back on Earth for a little while though, their bones strengthened again. Nowadays, astronauts are encouraged to use exercise machines in the spacecraft to prevent their bones from losing calcium.

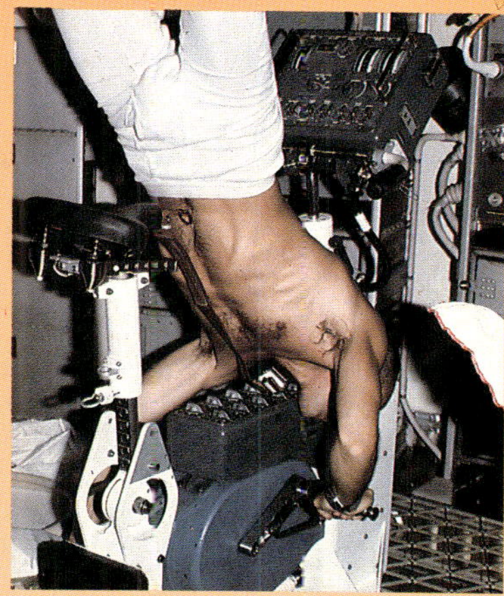

Astronaut pedalling upside-down on an exercise machine in space

Body defence systems

Your body is like a battlefield. Every moment of your life, your body is on guard against harmful bacteria — the germs that make you ill. Again and again, your body wins battles against these invaders without you ever knowing. Sometimes, though, the battles are hard fought and make you feel ill.

The most important defence we have against infection from harmful bacteria is our skin. This layer of cells keeps bacteria away from our more vulnerable cells. This is why we must keep our skin clean and ensure that any damage to it is repaired as soon as possible. Our eyelashes and eyelids also play a part in the defence against attack as do the small hairs and mucus in our nose.

You see one way the body fights infection when you cut yourself. A scab quickly forms on the wound. At first it is jelly-like but then it hardens to a crust to close and shield the cut. The scab is made from tiny discs of blood which stick together and become trapped in a mass of fibres. New skin grows under the scab. If you knock the scab off, it has to form again and the cut takes longer to heal.

Our blood is made up of a liquid called plasma and two kinds of cells — the red cells which carry the oxygen and the white cells which protect against infection. There are two types of white cell — one type attacks germs and the bacteria that may enter the body and the other produces antibodies which help protect us from disease. White blood cells collect near cuts and wounds to stop bacteria entering the body.

Dr Edward Jenner –

his discovery of a smallpox vaccine

Smallpox was a disease that used to kill and badly scar people by the million. It killed rich and poor people, the old and the young, babies and small children. Smallpox was killing people in China, Egypt and the Middle East 3000 years ago. Over the centuries, it spread throughout the world.

It is reckoned that 60 million people died from this dreadful disease in Europe in the 18th century. Most people who caught smallpox didn't die but they were often left blind, deaf, crippled or brain-damaged by the disease. Everyone who had had smallpox bore the terrible scars on their skin. There was no cure.

Even as recently as 1965, 10 to 15 million people in 33 countries caught smallpox and two million died. But the last case of smallpox in the world was in 1978. The disease has been defeated. The long chain of human misery stretching back thousands of years was finally broken.

The man who discovered how to defeat smallpox lived and worked as a doctor in Gloucestershire about 200 years ago. His name was Edward Jenner. As well as caring for his patients, he wrote poems, studied chemistry and was very interested in nature. He carefully examined dead animals to learn about their diseases. He was extremely good at observing and believed in finding out answers to problems by doing experiments. Edward Jenner used the skills of collecting evidence, observing and experimenting to discover the cure for smallpox.

Edward Jenner knew that people who survived smallpox didn't catch it again. Some people even tried to give themselves a mild attack of smallpox to try to protect themselves from a more serious attack which they might catch later. In China some doctors blew ground-up scab into a patient's nostrils. That didn't work. In Turkey, Ethiopia and India, bits of scab or pus from a smallpox sore were put into a scratch made in a healthy person's skin. If the person was lucky, this resulted in a mild attack of smallpox and immunity from the disease for life.

An English woman, Lady Mary Wortley Montagu, watched this method of 'inoculating' against smallpox being used in Turkey. She persuaded people back home in England to try it. 'Inoculation' seemed to work but the technique had to be carried out very carefully and people were careless. Often a bad attack of smallpox followed. Smallpox was so infectious that even a mild attack spread the disease. More and more people died.

When he was about 12, Edward Jenner began working for a country doctor as his apprentice. When visiting a farm on his rounds, he heard a milkmaid talking to a friend.

Cowpox came from cows which were infected with sores. People milking these cows found that they often developed similar sores on their hands. They recovered from cowpox quite easily but began to realize that having had cowpox meant that they were unlikely to catch smallpox. Unfortunately, many doctors thought the farmworkers were stupid and didn't even bother to check what they were saying.

Edward Jenner, however, remembered what the milkmaid had said and began to study the link between cowpox and smallpox. He collected as much information as he could and talked to many people who said they had caught cowpox in the past. For a long time, though, he couldn't find anyone who could show him the cowpox sores on their hands.

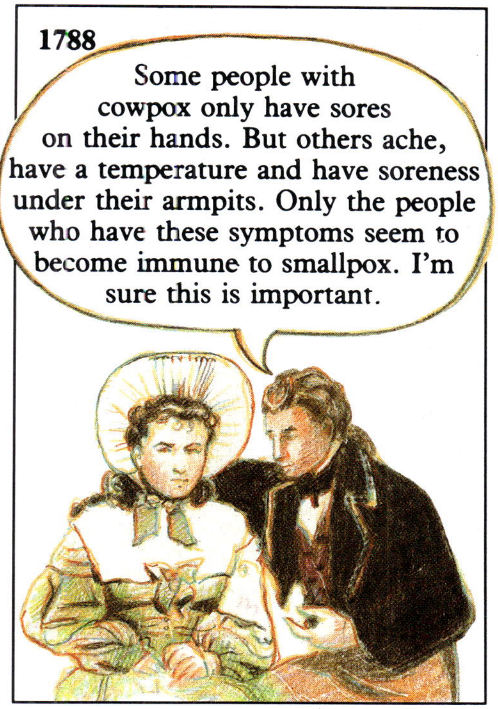

April 1795
This is Joseph Merret. He had true cowpox 25 years ago. I have tried to give him smallpox but he hasn't caught it. His whole family had smallpox but not Joseph.
But how do you know he didn't have smallpox when he was a child?
Because this is a village and everyone knows everyone else's business!
Christmas 1795
I have made a list of people who have had cowpox in the past. None of them can be made to catch smallpox. I am ready to try my experiment but first I need to find someone who has got cowpox now.
May 1796
I scratched my hand on a thorn, sir. Now I've got the cowpox from my master's cows. The sore has come in the place where the scratch happened.
14 May 1796
I'm going to make two little scratches on your arm. You are a healthy boy, James Phipps, and you'll come to no harm.
I'll put some of the material which I have taken from the sore on Sarah Nelmes' hand into his scratches. This will inoculate your boy with cowpox and I think it will protect him from smallpox.
23 May 1796
You say you have a headache and you don't want to eat? You feel a little chilled? That's all as I expected. You have a very mild attack of cowpox. The sores will soon go.

Jenner could not do any more experiments for the next two years because there was no cowpox on the farms. When cowpox came back to the local cows, Jenner checked his discovery by inoculating more children. None could be made to get even a mild attack of smallpox.

Jenner wrote a book about his research and experiments and how to use cowpox for inoculating. The book changed human history.

Edward Jenner had found the first truly safe and effective way of preventing people from catching smallpox. But 200 years ago, few people understood what infectious diseases were or how they happened. Jenner knew he could only convince people by proof. For months he tried to persuade doctors in London to try his new technique. Finally, one doctor at a London hospital used the cowpox inoculation on a boy. It worked.

Some doctors refused to believe it was possible but, nevertheless, the news that smallpox could at last be attacked spread fast throughout the world. The Emperor Napoleon of France quickly understood how important inoculation would be to the health of his army and navy, and ordered all his troops to be inoculated with the cowpox vaccine. The President of the United States inoculated his family, relations and neighbours and began inoculating local Indians.

But smallpox still spread. Some countries were too poor to pay for inoculation programmes. Others didn't make the smallpox vaccination compulsory. The British Government did not make smallpox vaccination compulsory until 1853 — 57 years after Jenner's discovery.

Now, after huge organization and effort, smallpox has gone. Billions of people have been vaccinated by having a little of the cowpox virus put into them — the method worked out by Edward Jenner in Gloucestershire, 200 years ago.

A healthy diet builds healthy bodies

Your body is growing and being re-built continuously. You build yourself up from the food you eat. Just like any type of building, it is important to use the right materials. To have a strong, healthy body you need regular meals and a well-balanced diet. Each day's food should include six important ingredients: proteins, carbohydrates, fats, minerals, vitamins and fibre. These ingredients are all needed to enable the body to convert protein into substances which are used to build new cells. Whenever you can, try and choose foods which contain these ingredients.

There is a lot of body-building protein in the animal products, meat, fish, milk and eggs and also a smaller amount in certain nuts, beans, peas and cereal grains.

Carbohydrate gives you energy. It comes from the starch and sugar you eat in bread, potatoes, cereal, fruit and nuts. Pasta is a good source of carbohydrate. Many marathon runners eat a big pasta meal the evening before a race to give them extra energy. There is plenty of carbohydrate in cakes, biscuits and sweets too but it comes in a form that is more likely to make you fat than fit — and it ruins your teeth if you don't brush them regularly.

Fat also gives you energy and it contains some vital chemicals that keep the body working properly. You eat fat in meat, milk, butter, oil, nuts and certain vegetables.

None of the body-building foods can be used properly unless you also eat certain minerals. These include calcium, phosphorus and magnesium and they come mainly from milk and dairy products such as butter, cheese, yoghurt and dairy ice-cream. Seafood and some green vegetables contain minerals as well. Calcium is needed particularly to build healthy bones and teeth. Your bones can only absorb this calcium properly if you take in other minerals and vitamins as well.

Foods containing Vitamin C

Foods containing protein

Foods containing carbohydrate

Foods containing minerals

Foods containing fat

Foods containing Vitamin A

A fresh supply of vitamins each day is important:

- Vitamin A helps bone growth and also helps vision in conditions when there isn't much light. It is found in carrots and yellow fruits and vegetables and also in milk and liver.
- Vitamin C is needed to produce the stringy fibres in your bones, and especially to mend fractures. You are unlikely to get Vitamin C unless you eat at least some fresh fruit and vegetables especially citrus fruits and green leafy vegetables.
- Vitamin D is needed for bones to harden properly. It is found in fatty foods such as milk, cheese, eggs, oily fish and liver. Sunshine helps to provide Vitamin D by changing fats in the skin.

There are some things that make your bones lose some of their calcium. Alcohol and nicotine from cigarettes are two of them and this is just one reason why everyone should avoid taking them, particularly young children. Caffeine in tea and coffee, chocolate, sugar, bran and red meat also reduce calcium absorption. However, bran and red meat are healthy foods in other ways.

Foods containing Vitamin D

Digestion

Before food can be absorbed by cells in the body, it must be broken down into a solution that can be carried by the blood. This process is called digestion.

Digestion starts in the mouth. We chew our food, grinding and breaking it up into smaller bits and particles with our teeth. At the same time, our saliva acts on and starts to take out some of the useful parts of the food. When we swallow the chewed food, it passes into our stomach where the main digestion takes place. There, the food is mixed with digestive juices made up of acids and other chemicals, and churned up until most of the useful substances are in a solution. It is then passed into our intestine from where it is absorbed into our blood and transported around our body to the cells. The unused, wasted food is excreted later.

Mouth
The mouth is where food is chewed and mixed with saliva.

Liver
The liver is the chemical factory of the body that processes the blood carrying the dissolved solutions from the intestine.

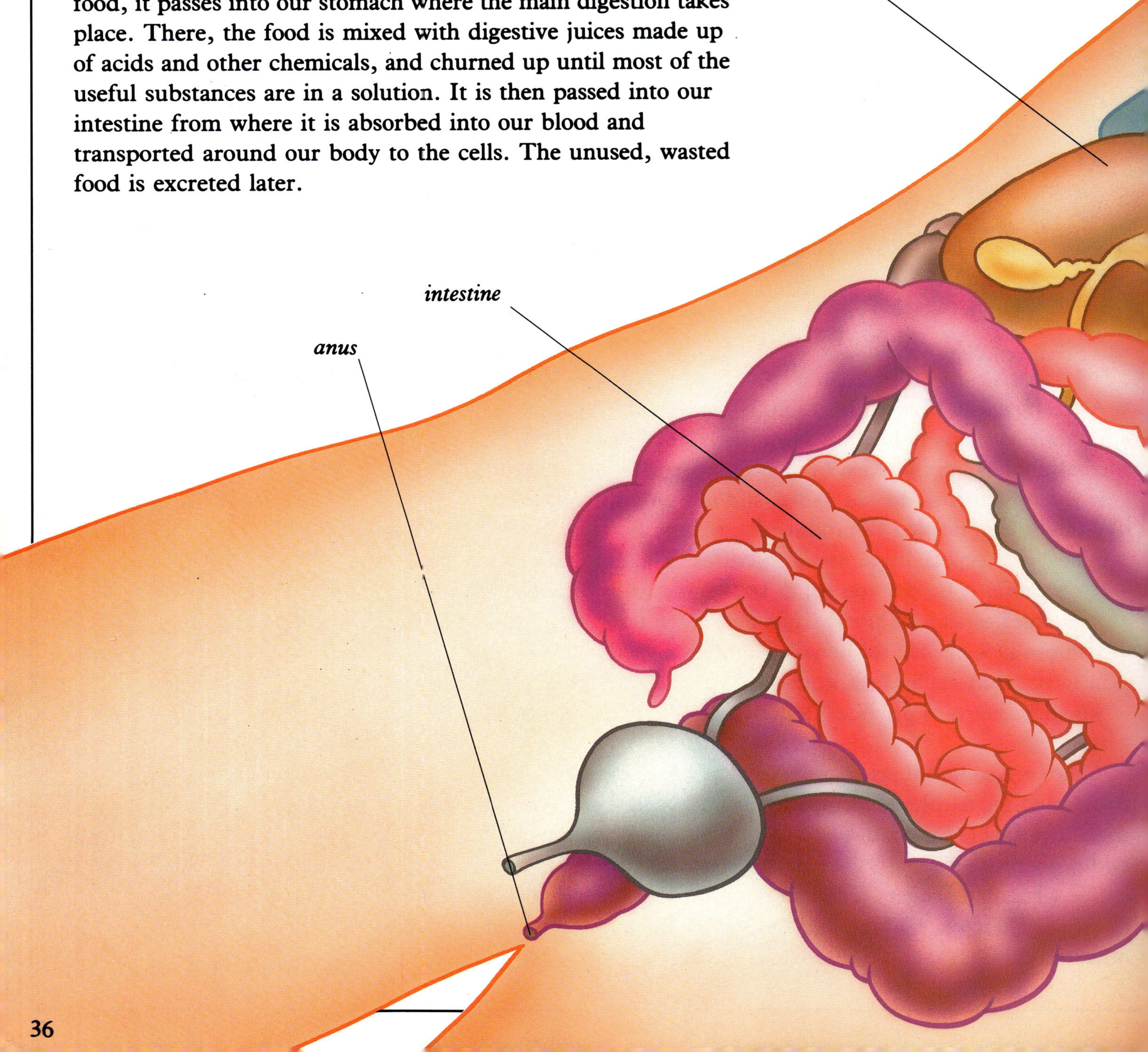

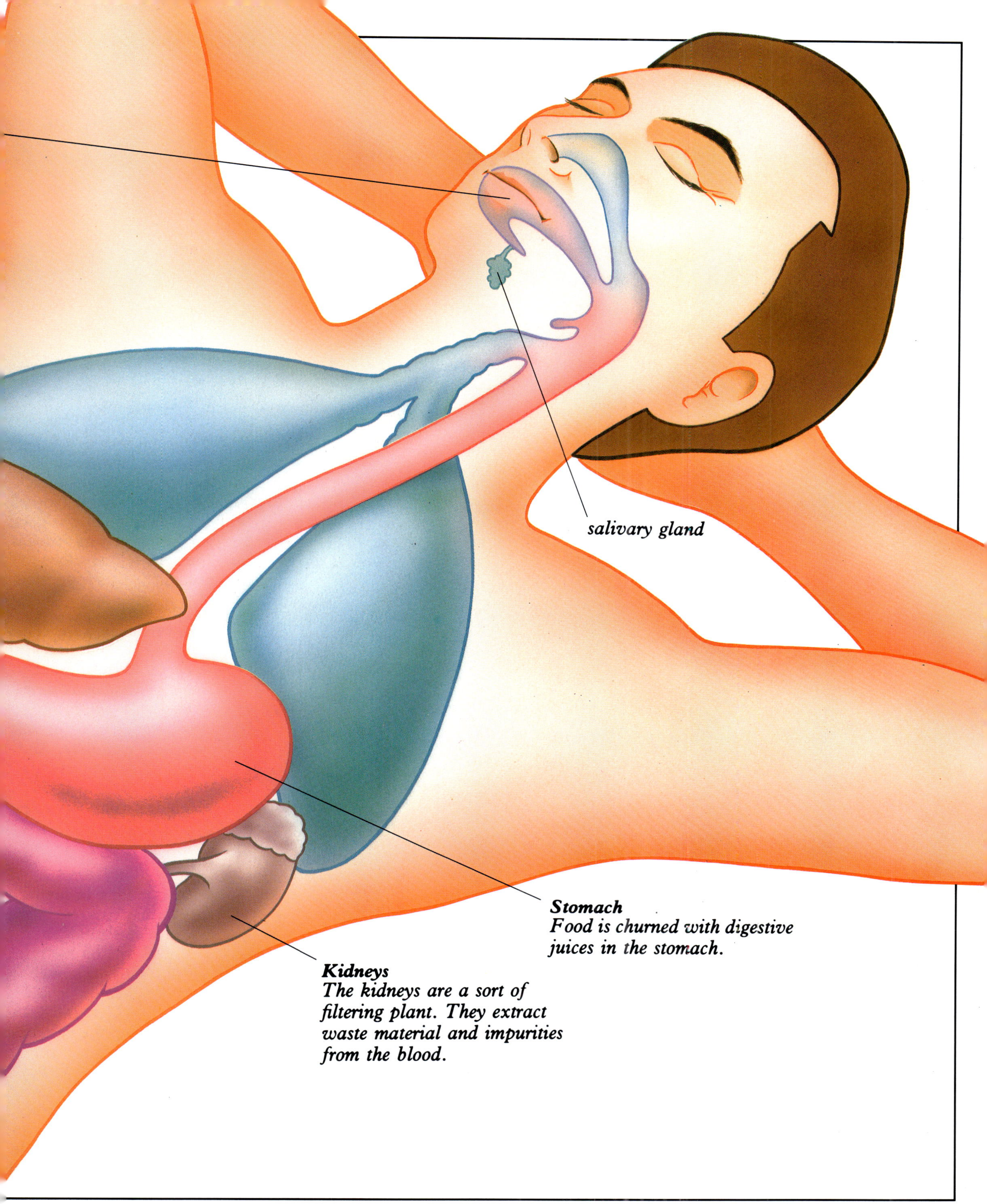
salivary gland
Stomach
Food is churned with digestive juices in the stomach.
Kidneys
The kidneys are a sort of filtering plant. They extract waste material and impurities from the blood.

Body Works Ltd
MUSCLE & BONE
COMPLAINTS DEPARTMENT
I want to make a complaint about my back. It just won't stop aching.
Well Mr Spiney, I'm afraid backache is a very common complaint and all I can do is offer you some advice. You must be careful at work when you're lifting all those heavy boxes in the supermarket warehouse. Always use the strength of your hip and leg muscles to help you, not just your arms and shoulders. And always keep a good posture whatever you're doing. Sleep on a firm bed without too many pillows.
I'm always being encouraged to take more exercise so last night I played 5-a-side football with some friends. It was good fun but I kept getting stitches and cramp. I felt so silly because all the others seemed so fit.
I'm sure they were. They play every week and are quite used to so much exercise in a short time. You have to build up your stamina and muscle strength gradually. And before you take any exercise, you must do some warm-up exercises.
I can't understand it — when I was younger I was 5 feet 6 but now I'm only 5 feet 5.
So talking in metric terms, you reckon you've shrunk from 1.68 to 1.65 metres. Actually, that is possible. As people grow older, the discs between the vertebrae in their spines get thinner so that they actually shrink in height. Their spines also tend to curve so that some old people look rather short and bowed.

I've got a lot of pain in my right leg. I don't know what I've done to it to make it hurt so much.
Looking at it, I don't believe you've actually hurt your leg at all although there is some swelling there. I think it's your back that's causing the problem. I suspect you're suffering from sciatica. This happens when one of the discs between the vertebrae in the spine slips out of place. The disc presses on a nerve which runs up through the spine but causes pain to be felt in the leg.
here, does that feel better? I've ushed your bones back in place. I now it was very painful at the time. ou had dislocated the bones in your houlder joint so that they had come ut of position. You should be OK ow.
Yes, that's much better. I'll certainly take more care when I dive into the pool next time.
ly wrist really urts.
I think you may have fallen so heavily on your wrist that you've torn a ligament in your joint. If that's the case, I'm afraid you won't be playing volleyball again for a little while — not until your wrist joint is strong enough.
Grandad, will you play football with me?
I'll try, Tessa, but I'm not as quick as I used to be. My joints are so stiff. It's getting old that does it. My doctor says the rubbing surfaces on my bones have worn out. He's promised me a new knee joint next year, made of stainless steel. Then you'd better watch out, Tessa. I might be as quick as you are again!

Helping hands

Mrs Kennedy suffers from arthritis, a condition which causes painful swelling of the joints. Arthritis does affect young people but is much more common amongst elderly people. Arthritis makes movements of many kinds very difficult.

Mrs Kennedy manages to live on her own still because of the range of tools and gadgets that have been developed to help people like her. These pictures of Mrs Kennedy at home show some of the ways in which her life has been made easier.

This kitchen is a real help. The special taps mean that I can turn them on so much more easily than normal ones. The cupboard doors are magnetic — they just pop open when I push them. The cooker is electric which is safer for me, especially if I have trouble turning the power off. I use the microwave a lot now though. I buy ready-scrubbed vegetables and pop them in for a minute or two. After I have eaten I just stack everything carefully in the dishwasher which I bought recently. I found it hard to grip on to wet plates properly when I used to have to wash up by hand.

I usually have a shower because it's so much easier than climbing into a bath. I usually shower sitting down so that I don't slip over. The handrail by the toilet is to steady me when I sit down or stand up.

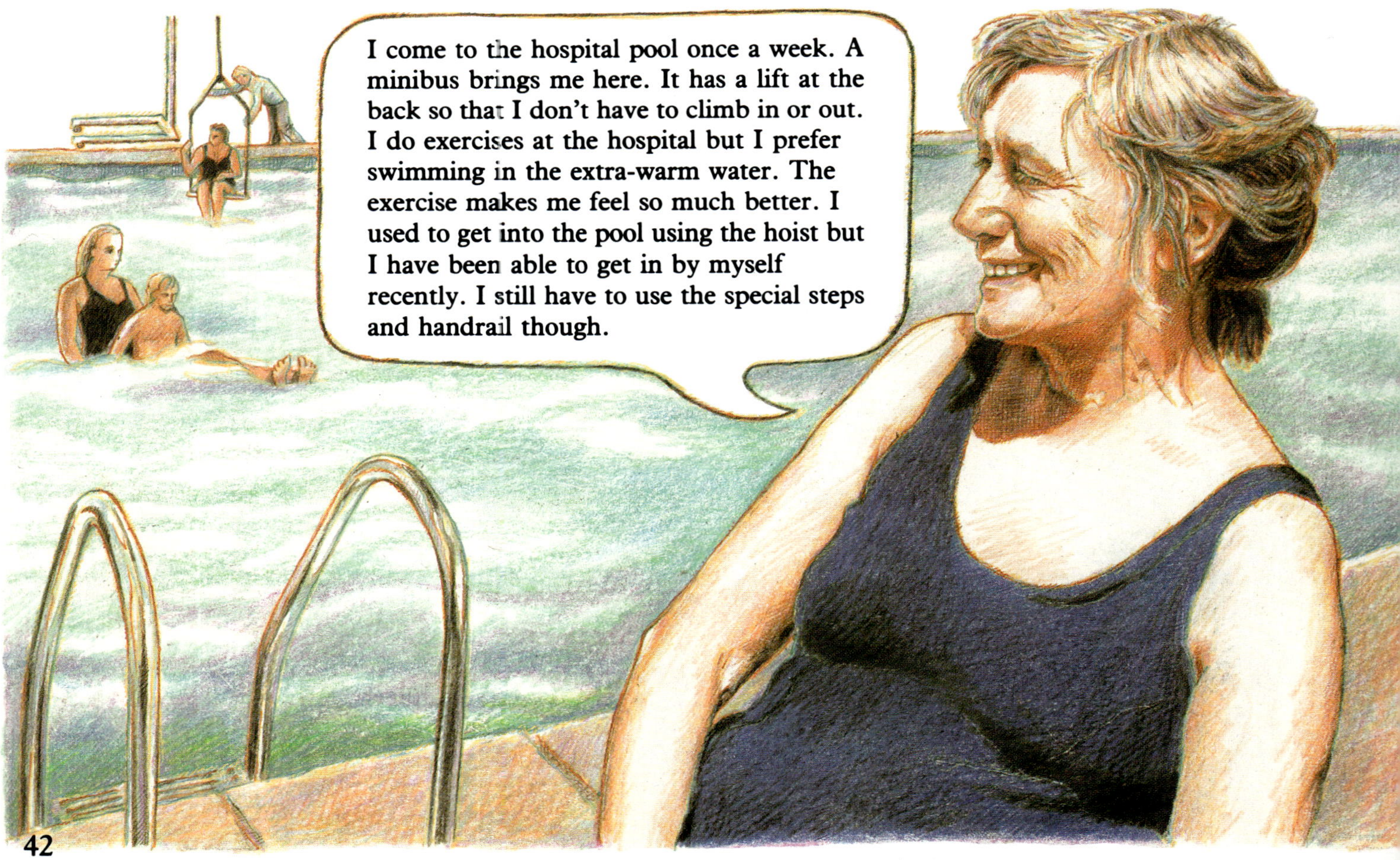
I come to the hospital pool once a week. A minibus brings me here. It has a lift at the back so that I don't have to climb in or out. I do exercises at the hospital but I prefer swimming in the extra-warm water. The exercise makes me feel so much better. I used to get into the pool using the hoist but I have been able to get in by myself recently. I still have to use the special steps and handrail though.

My Gramp

My gramp has got a medal.
On the front there is a runner.
On the back it says:
Senior Boys 100 Yards
First William Green
I asked him about it,
but before he could reply
Gran said, 'Don't listen to his tales.
The only running he ever did
was after the girls.'
Gramp gave a chuckle
and went out the back
to get the tea.
As he shuffled down the passage
with his back bent,
I tried to imagine him,
legs flying, chest out,
breasting the tape.
But I couldn't.

John Foster

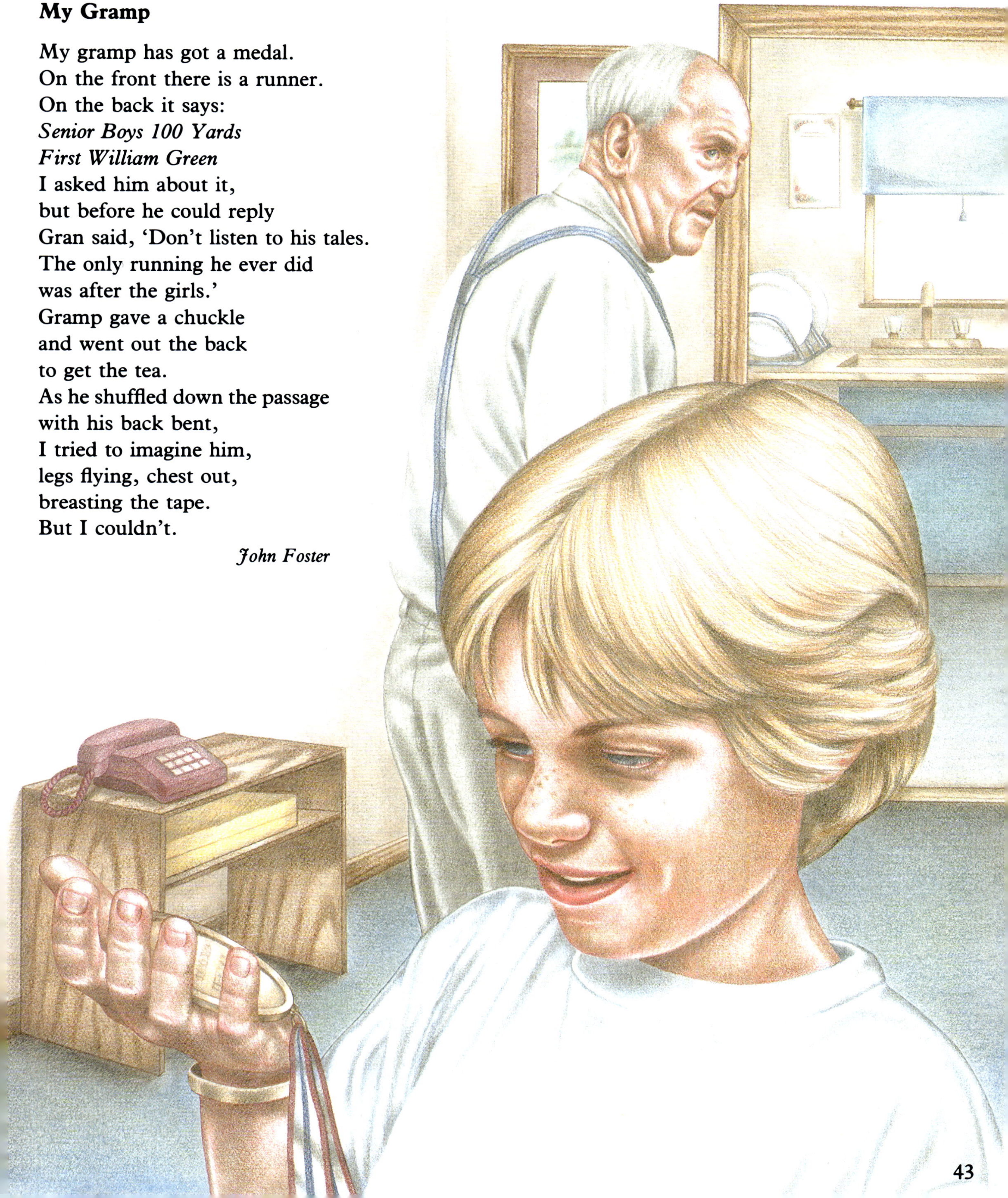

Smoking and drinking

Lots of people smoke and lots of people drink — not just water or fruit juice but drinks like beer, whisky or gin. For others, there is nothing better than a 'nice cup of tea or coffee'.

Most people smoke or drink these things because it seems to make them feel better, more relaxed. When people are nervous a cigarette sometimes seems to calm them down; after a hard day's work a drink seems to reduce their troubles and stress.

Tobacco and certain kinds of drink can make people feel calm because they contain drugs which affect the ways in which our bodies work. For a time, these drugs cause pleasant sensations. Unfortunately, they have effects on us which we don't realize. Little by little, the drugs in cigarettes and some of our drinks can prove to be very harmful.

Coffee and tea, for example, contain a drug called caffeine. Caffeine is **addictive** — after a while your body begins to really need it; you seem to have no choice in the matter. The more you have, the more you want. If caffeine wasn't harmful, this might not matter but caffeine is harmful. The more caffeine you put into your body, the less relaxed you become; caffeine makes you nervous and irritable. That's why so many more people are now trying to change to coffee without caffeine which is called decaffeinated coffee.

Two hundred years ago there were public coffee houses like the one in the picture below, where people would meet to drink coffee and talk about their business.

Cigarettes and cigars contain a drug called nicotine. Nicotine is a very addictive drug too. Many people find it impossible just to have one or two cigarettes. They have to smoke them all the time. Becoming addicted to cigarettes is very serious. You may remember from the Year 5 Ginn Science book called 'Body Business' that cigarettes also contain other harmful substances as well as the drug nicotine. As people smoke cigarettes, they breathe in things which will probably cause great damage to their bodies. Sticky black tar can clog up their lungs and blood vessels making them weak and breathless. Other substances can cause lung and heart disease and damage to arteries.

None of these things happens immediately; they take time. At first, smokers think that cigarettes are just enjoyable. They can't see or feel what is happening to them. Sometimes you will see sportsmen and women smoking who look really healthy but often they are still quite young and probably haven't been smoking that long. The important question is what will they be like in twenty years' time when the damage caused by cigarettes begins to show?

Beer, wines and spirit drinks such as whisky or vodka contain a drug called alcohol. Drinks like these make people feel more relaxed because the alcohol affects their brains. Too much alcohol begins to kill the cells in the brain; it literally stops the brain from working properly.

Too much alcohol can be very dangerous. You might have laughed at someone who appears to be drunk on television or someone you might have seen in the street. But drunks behave stupidly because the alcohol is damaging their brains, slowing them down and stopping them from thinking. A drunk driving a car down a busy street or a drunk involved in a vicious argument stops being funny when they kill or hurt people.

All of these drugs are particularly dangerous to children; they slow down growth and stop the brain from developing properly. Even unborn babies can be affected by the alcohol, nicotine or caffeine taken in by their mother. The moment you begin to take them, your body will begin to become addicted. Take care — look after yourself.

Drugs and medicines

A drug is any substance which affects the way in which your body works. Nicotine, caffeine and alchohol are drugs. Medicines are drugs too.

A medicine is a type of drug which helps to make your body work better. Medicines are drugs which have been designed to help you. However, medicines can be harmful to you if you use them when your body doesn't need them or if you take more than you should.

The dose — or amount — of medicine you take is very important. Too little and it won't help; too much and it could harm you. That is why the correct dose is always clearly stated on any bottle or packet of medicine you might have been given by the chemist or the doctor.

Medicines have helped transform many people's lives. Diabetics, for example, suffer from a disease in which sugar and starch are not properly absorbed from their blood. Nowadays, diabetics can take carefully controlled doses of a drug called insulin which helps to control the sugar levels in their blood. Epileptics can take drugs which prevent them becoming unconscious. People with high blood pressure can take tablets to reduce their blood pressure and the likelihood of their having heart attacks or strokes.

Most of us only need medicines to help us recover from particular short-term illnesses or accidents. That's the only time most of us would use them — when it is absolutely necessary. Like alcohol and nicotine, the drugs in many medicines can be addictive. Too much medicine can be very bad for you. When medicines are no longer needed, they should be thrown away carefully or returned to the chemist. All medicines should be kept out of reach of children.

Drugs trolley in a doctor's surgery

Chemist's shop

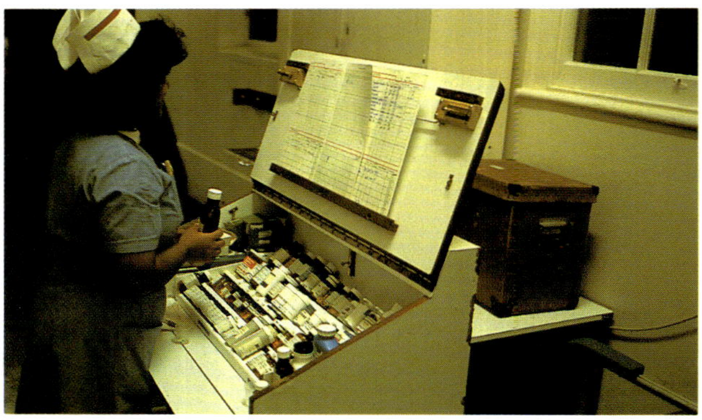

Nurse organizing medicines in a hospital ward

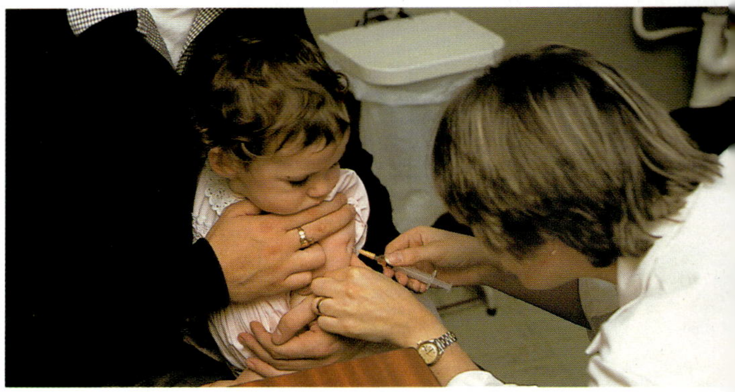

Baby having an injection

Illegal drugs

Medicines are drugs which have been carefully designed by scientists to help you when you are hurt or ill. Not all drugs are medicines, though; some just change the way your body works in a harmful way.

Alcohol, caffeine and nicotine affect your body harmfully but, for all sorts of reasons, many people don't seem to realize how harmful they can be. Other harmful drugs seem to cause us much more concern.

You have probably seen advertisements or television programmes warning against the use of drugs such as cocaine and heroin. These drugs are very dangerous. They are very addictive and, when you take them for the first few times, can make you feel really happy or lively — as though you haven't a care in the world. These feelings don't last though, and when they wear off the drugs affect your brain so that you feel unhappy and very depressed.

That's when you want to take the drug again and the circle begins — take the drug, feel happy and lively, feel very unhappy, take the drug, feel happy, feel very unhappy and so on. All the time the drug is making you want more and more. Soon, it becomes almost impossible to stop taking the drug even if you want to; the drug has won.

People addicted to heroin, cocaine and other drugs such as the solvents in some glues, can become very ill. They can damage their skin, suffer brain damage and heart attacks and lose their appetites. Their bodies don't receive the goodness they need.

These drugs aren't medicines which make you feel better; they are simply drugs which change the way your body works, usually for the worse. That is why so much money is spent trying to stop people selling them, taking them or buying them. That is why these drugs are illegal.

We need to be very suspicious of any drugs. In particular, though, be very suspicious of all drugs which aren't medicines, including the drugs in drinks and cigarettes as well as the illegal drugs such as cocaine and heroin.

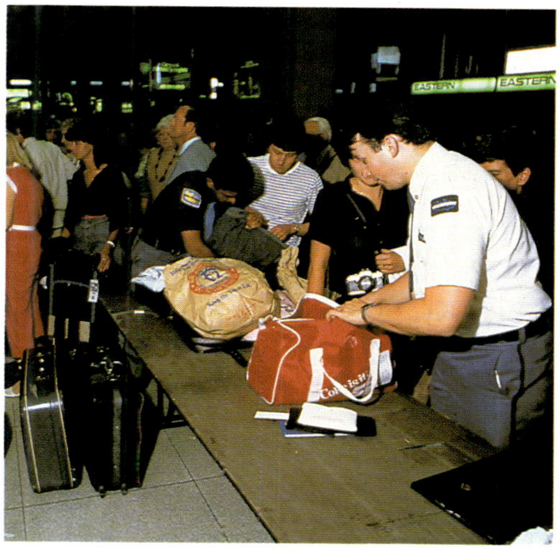

Security officers search the luggage of people at ports and airports to prevent them from bringing illegal drugs into the country.

Sniffer dog searching for illegal drugs

Glossary

addictive
An addictive substance is something on which you depend and which you cannot do without.

arthritis
Arthritis is the swelling of a joint which causes pain and stiffness.

cartilage
Cartilage is firm, flexible tissue normally found between bones in a joint where it acts as a cushion to prevent the bones rubbing together. Babies' bones begin as cartilage before gradually turning to bone.

chambers
Chambers are enclosed compartments or cavities in the body of an animal.

clot
A clot is a thick lump formed by blood when it begins to harden.

contracts
When something contracts, it becomes smaller or shorter.

digestion
Digestion is the process of breaking down foodstuffs to produce simpler substances that can be absorbed into the blood.

non-return valve
A non-return valve is a flap in an animal's body that ensures blood only flows in one direction.

respiration
Respiration is the process of taking in oxygen and releasing carbon dioxide.

Index